GEORGE W. BUSH

AN UNAUTHORIZED ORAL HISTORY

Tom Ruprecht

Andrews McMeel Publishing, LLC
Kansas City

 For information, write Andrews McMeel Publishing, LLC, an Andrews McMeel Universal company, 4520 Main Street, Kansas City, Missouri 64111.

07 08 09 10 11 MLT 10 9 8 7 6 5 4 3 2

ISBN-13: 978-0-7407-6757-9
ISBN-10: 0-7407-6757-7

Library of Congress Control Number: 2006937591

www.andrewsmcmeel.com

I'd like to dedicate this to my dad and the memory of my mom.

Oh, and also to Lindsay Lohan. Don't listen to the haters.
You know you're my #1 baby.

Contents

1

Bush's Infancy: 1946 to Present . . . 3

2

How to Get Through Yale without Learning a Damn Thing . . . 11

3

Vietnam: Those Who Got Cs in History
Are Doomed to Repeat It . . . 21

4

Just Your Typical Forty-Year-Old Slacker
Sponging Off Mom and Dad . . . 29

5

A Time When the World Respected
the Words "President Bush" . . . 39

6

Striking Out on His Own . . . 43

7

Before Schwarzenegger. Before Jesse "The Body."
The Original Embarrassing Governor . . . 47

8
Economy's Good, There's a Budget Surplus, America's at Peace ...
Yeah, the Country Needs a New Direction ... 55

9
Bush and Rove: The Two Men You Want Planning Your War ... 67

10
Mission Accomp ... Hey, What the Hell Happened?! ... 75

11
Letting New Orleans Get Washed Away and a
Couple Other Minor Bloopers ... 87

12
Road Trip! ... 93

13
Daddy Becomes Friends with Clinton:
A Disturbing Early Sign of Dementia? ... 103

14
Mission Accomp ... Wait, We *Still* Haven't Won This Thing?! ... 109

15
Vice Presidents Are Supposed to *Attend* Funerals,
Not Cause Them ... 119

16
"Hey, 16! Just Like My Approval Rating!" ... 125

Acknowledgments ... 133

George W. Bush:

An Unauthorized Oral History

CHAPTER 1

Bush's Infancy: 1946 to Present

You have to understand, back then it wasn't unusual for a woman to smoke during pregnancy. It was only later that we learned about the effects on the child's mental development.

BARBARA BUSH, FORMER FIRST LADY

I'LL NEVER FORGET the first time I held George and looked into his eyes. So lost, so helpless. I still see that same look whenever he talks about Iraq. [Laughs] You gotta watch out for me. The old guy loves giving you the needle.

GEORGE H. W. BUSH, FORMER PRESIDENT

[Rolling her eyes] "The needle." Ah yes, the patented towel-snapping humor of the Bush men. Well, did my hilarious husband tell you where he was when he first looked into our new son's eyes? Or when? George didn't see our son until I brought him home from the hospital five days later. You see, my husband refused to visit because he says hospitals make him queasy. He has a very weak stomach—as the president of Japan discovered.

Barbara Bush, FORMER FIRST LADY

SHE TOLD YOU THAT? [Stares out the window and shakes his head] She's a rough one, boy. They call her "The Silver Fox," you know. Well, you may want to inform my wife that I threw up on the Japanese prime minister, not the Japanese president.

George H. W. Bush, FORMER PRESIDENT

Oh well, that's much better.

Barbara Bush, FORMER FIRST LADY

IT'S A PRETTY BIG HONOR to say you delivered a future president of the United States. I got to smack George W. Bush on the behind. How much do you think Teddy Kennedy would pay for the chance to do that? [Laughs] I like to tell that one on the practice tee; it really loosens everybody up.

Dr. Craig Thomas, OBGYN

Look, we'll get back to the birth of my son in a minute, but I just want to clear something up. There are many, *many* world leaders I never threw up on. Margaret Thatcher. Mikhail Gorbachev. Pierre Trudeau. Oh God, Trudeau; there's a guy I would've *loved* to have thrown up on, but I held back.

George H. W. Bush, FORMER PRESIDENT

NICE PEOPLE, THE BUSHES. This was over sixty years ago, but Barbara had gray hair even back then. I remember there were a bunch of newspaper reporters hanging around outside the delivery room. They thought they'd get to do one of those "Grandmother Has Baby" human interest stories until they found out she was only twenty-two. The husband never came inside. Just stood out in the parking lot all day looking queasy. Good guy, though. I contributed money to his campaign in '88 when he ran against that dago Dukakis. [Editor's note: Former governor Michael Dukakis is of Greek descent. He is not a "dago."]

DR. CRAIG THOMAS, OBGYN

George was born in 1946. I remember that as being a really wonderful time in America. The war was over, the economy was booming, colored people had to use separate water fountains. You really felt like the country was headed in the right direction. Unlike, say, now.

BARBARA BUSH, FORMER FIRST LADY

AH, HERE IT IS! [Holds up a photo] That's a picture of former President Bush and me at a fund-raiser. See how he signed it? "Thanks for the 'special delivery'!" [Laughs] Get it? 'Cuz I delivered his boy. [Looking around] Say, if you see our waitress, I could use another gin and tonic.

DR. CRAIG THOMAS, OBGYN

George was born almost exactly nine months after Barbara and I started trying to have a child. How 'bout that?! Ol' George works pretty quick, huh?! Who's the wimp now? Did Reagan knock up his wife that quick? Or how 'bout that dago Dukakis?

George H. W. Bush, FORMER PRESIDENT

Uh, yeah, it was about nine months. Six months, nine months. Who's counting? Besides, they say it's normal for your first baby to come several months premature.

Barbara Bush, FORMER FIRST LADY

When George was teething, he'd cry so much. I'd try and soothe him by letting him suck on a rag that was soaked in whiskey. Oh how he loved sucking on that whiskey rag! We started to get suspicious around the time George turned fourteen and still claimed to be teething.

Barbara Bush, FORMER FIRST LADY

I was away a lot when George was a boy. I was busy with the oil business and then I served as ambassador to China. I felt bad about missing so much of his childhood.

George H. W. Bush, FORMER PRESIDENT

Because he wasn't around a lot, my husband tried to compensate by buying lots of toys, which I think young George viewed as sort of a "win-win."

Barbara Bush, FORMER FIRST LADY

GEORGE GOT FIFTY CENTS a week for allowance. We tried to teach him the value of saving money. Now I look at how he turned a $284 billion surplus into a $412 billion deficit and I just wanna freakin' kill myself. What kind of parents were we? Of course, I wasn't around a lot, so it's mostly Barbara's fault.

GEORGE H. W. BUSH, FORMER PRESIDENT

The '50s were a magical time to be a kid. I remember I'd save my allowance and on Saturday afternoons I'd take the train to Yankee Stadium. I'd buy a bleacher seat for a nickel. Usually when I'd reach into my pockets, I'd find that Grandpa had snuck me an extra nickel to buy a hot dog. One day Mickey Mantle hit a homer and when he got back to the outfield, he winked right at me! During the winters, I'd take the train to Times Square and see a Tarzan movie at the old Rialto.

BILLY CRYSTAL, COMEDIAN

[Editor's note: When we tried to explain that the stories had to be about George W. Bush, Mr. Crystal simply launched into another one about how on Sunday nights his grandpa would pay Billy a nickel to do his Sammy Davis Jr. impression in the living room. So we finally agreed to publish this just to shut him up.]

GEORGE WAS ONE OF MY STUDENTS. I remember how eager he was to learn. He'd sit right in the front row. His eyes were always wide open as if he was trying to soak in every last bit of information. [Stares at photo of the class] Oh, wait; I'm sorry, I was thinking of Bradley Meeker, the boy who sat in front of George. The Bush kid? Yeah, he was a dumbass.

PAT LIONETTI, THIRD-GRADE TEACHER

George was absent from class the day we discussed the history of ethnic conflict in the Middle East. Didn't seem like a big deal at the time.

Dean Sluyter, FIFTH-GRADE HISTORY TEACHER

Hey there, Ike-a-maniacs! While campaigning in Houston, I was approached by a ten-year-old boy. He held his arms akimbo and walked up to me with an exaggerated swagger. He said his name was "George W." and that one day he was going to be a president, too. What a cocky twerp. I swear, I have no patience for that kind of crap. I mean, I had to defeat Hitler—Adolf freakin' Hitler, worst guy in the world—to get myself elected president. And now some little nerd is telling me *he's* presidential timber? So I started kicking him in the shins. Well, as I was kicking him, his mother came over and asked me for an autograph. I started to sign a piece of paper, but get this, Ike-a-maniacs—she told me to sign her breast!

EXCERPT FROM DWIGHT D. EISENHOWER'S
1957 AUTOBIOGRAPHY *IKE-A-MANIA*

I'm not a jealous guy, but I wasn't wild about Eisenhower signing my wife's breast. To make it worse, Barbara didn't wash it for weeks. Every night when I crawled into bed, I had to see "Dwight D. Eisenhower" scrawled on my wife's bosom—like a living veto of our marriage.

George H. W. Bush, FORMER PRESIDENT

My husband had been captain of his college baseball team, so little George was very excited when he started Little League. He wanted to be a ballplayer just like his father.

Barbara Bush, FORMER FIRST LADY

Don't make any comparison between my baseball career and his. Don't go there. The kid was awful.

GEORGE H. W. BUSH, FORMER PRESIDENT

MY HUSBAND used to bet against Georgie's team whenever the boy pitched. And these weren't small bets; it was thousands of dollars a game. Against his own son.

BARBARA BUSH, FORMER FIRST LADY

Yup. I did do that. [Chuckles] Oh, he'd just get murdered. But hey, some of the money I won I later used to help rig the 2000 election, so, you know, it was sort of an act of love.

GEORGE H. W. BUSH, FORMER PRESIDENT

GEORGE HAD A LITTLE TROUBLE finding something that caught his interest in school. He floundered from club to club. It seemed everything he tried to do, he invariably failed where his father succeeded. Then in seventh grade he heard about the National Spelling Bee. Finally, he felt like he'd found his own interest.

DON MACKINNON, ANDOVER GUIDANCE COUNSELOR

Remember, these were the days before you had all those brainiacs coming over from India in rickshaws making our schools look like Calcutta High. So a white kid still had a chance in a spelling bee.

BARBARA BUSH, FORMER FIRST LADY

GEORGE STUDIED THAT DICTIONARY day and night. For the first and only time in his life, I was almost proud of him.

GEORGE H. W. BUSH, FORMER PRESIDENT

Mr. and Mrs. Bush were so excited that something had finally sparked George's interest. So they spared no expense trying to prepare him for the competition. They hired a Latin tutor and a Greek tutor to help George with etymologies. They bought him a beautiful leather-bound dictionary. It was very exciting.

DON MACKINNON, ANDOVER GUIDANCE COUNSELOR

GEORGE WORKED SO HARD. For months. And then he went to the gymnasium for the big event. September 26th. I still remember the date. I didn't want to get overconfident, but I really thought he had a chance to win the whole thing.

BARBARA BUSH, FORMER FIRST LADY

The dumbass got eliminated on his first word: "shovel." I spent $7,000 on tutors and the dimwit couldn't even spell "shovel." I'm actually not surprised. He probably heard "shovel" and immediately panicked that he might have to do manual labor. If they'd given him a word like "hammock" or "Popsicle," he would've done much better.

GEORGE H. W. BUSH, FORMER PRESIDENT

CHAPTER 2

How to Get Through Yale without Learning a Damn Thing

When George got to high school, he still hadn't given up his dream of being a baseball player.

Barbara Bush, FORMER FIRST LADY

He tried out for the team, but George was an absolute klutz. We have a term in baseball: "sucked." George sucked.

Jerry Foley, ANDOVER BASEBALL COACH

My husband and I tried to pull some strings to get little George on the team, but it turns out it's easier to bribe your kid into the White House than a high school baseball team.

Barbara Bush, FORMER FIRST LADY

Because he couldn't play baseball, George did the next best thing—he became a male cheerleader. Oh wait, did I say "next best thing"? I meant "the most pansy-assed thing imaginable." A male cheerleader?! What an embarrassment. I would've been prouder if he quit going to class and became a junkie, which is pretty much what he did in college, by the way, but I'm getting ahead of myself.

George H. W. Bush, FORMER PRESIDENT

As it is with cheerleaders at many schools, one of George's responsibilities was to "make it" with the quarterback before a big game. You don't exactly have to be Freud to figure out why he's now leading the fight against gay marriage.

Alden Provost, ANDOVER CLASSMATE

I WAS WORKING IN THE OIL FIELDS of Odessa one day when a guy on the crew starts telling everybody that my son is a cheerleader. Sweet Jesus, it was a nightmare! Worst day of my life—and that's coming from a guy who had his freakin' plane shot down over the Pacific.

George H. W. Bush, FORMER PRESIDENT

George was sort of the class clown. So when he became a cheerleader, he showed up one day wearing a girl's cheerleading outfit. Short skirt, lipstick, bra with padding. Okay fine, whatever. But then he wore it the next day. And the next. And the next. And he kept doing it. I mean, by February it was kinda like, "Hey George, joke's over."

Alden Provost, ANDOVER CLASSMATE

He was a male cheerleader; I'm a decorated war hero. And yet somehow *I'm* the wimp?! Good Christ, can someone explain that to me?

George H. W. Bush, former president

I went to that crappy boarding school. Full of phonies if you ask me. I met ol' Georgie boy in the waiting room for the school shrink. Ol' Bushie was sane as a goddamn baboon to tell you the truth. He was going on about his family. He said, "Do you know who I am?" meaning his dad was a big shot and all. I said, "Yeah, you're that faggy cheerleader." Well, he got all sore. He looked at me all Humphrey Bogart tough guy and said there'd be repercussions for what I said. "Repercussions!" Oh, that killed me.

Caulden Holyfield, Andover classmate

Of course, I can't think of that time without remembering the terrible Friday afternoon senior year when President Kennedy was shot. For people our age, it's one of the most significant moments of our lives. I remember years later asking George where he was when he heard the news. George said he was at a New Year's Eve party, which was a little odd because Kennedy was shot in November. But then again, George was never big on reading the newspaper.

Alden Provost, Andover classmate

The night of graduation, ol' Georgie came up to me and started hugging me like a goddamn madman. I looked at his face and he had tears in his eyes for Chrissake! I said five words to the guy outside a shrink's office and now he's blubbering like Sally Field in goddamn *Steel Magnolias* because we're saying good-bye? What a crazy phony! I almost sort of miss him to tell you the truth. That's the thing about people. A guy can act like a terrific phony for four years and then he hugs you with tears in his eyes on the night of graduation from some stupid school and that almost makes you sort of sorry to leave.

Caulden Holyfield, ANDOVER CLASSMATE

THE GUY YOU SHOULD REALLY TALK TO is Clayton Baxter. He was George's roommate through prep school and college. He and George were very good friends. He might be tough to track down, however. Last I heard, he was in Pakistan.

Alden Provost, ANDOVER CLASSMATE

I can't believe you found me! Well, sure I'll tell you about the times George and I had. Look, there were many things about Yale that I found undesirable—the gals at Kappa Alpha Theta for instance! Allah help me, *those* women should've been covered in veils. But one thing Yale *was* great for was networking. George introduced me to some of his dad's Saudi friends at a Christmas party and from that I got a job after college working for al-Qaeda.

Muhammad Al-Zadr (NÉ "CLAYTON BAXTER"),
FORMER BUSH ROOMMATE AT ANDOVER AND YALE

IT TOTALLY FEELS WEIRD doing this interview. For an infidel American book no less! But al-Qaeda's new publicist told me it'd be a good idea. (I know, I know. We finally broke down and got ourselves a publicist. Pretty soon the publicists will have publicists, right? But seriously, she's really good; she's Britney Spears's flack, so working for us is probably a picnic.) Anyhoo, she thinks al-Qaeda is losing out on the book-buying demographic—maybe it has something to do with the fact that we execute any girls caught reading, ha!—and so she feels this might help get our name out there.

Muhammad Al-Zadr (né "Clayton Baxter"), former Bush roommate at Andover and Yale

---

I honestly think if George knew about the "no reading" thing when we were back in school, he would've joined al-Qaeda in a second! Actually maybe al-Qaeda should send recruiters to college campuses like Goldman Sachs does and play up the "no reading" angle to the frat boys. [Pulls out a BlackBerry] Excuse me, I don't wanna lose that thought.

Muhammad Al-Zadr (né "Clayton Baxter"), former Bush roommate at Andover and Yale

---

[Admiring his BlackBerry] Aren't these things the best? I'm totally addicted. Osama calls it a "CrackBerry." I heard they used that line on *Entourage*, but they totally stole it from Osama.

Muhammad Al-Zadr (né "Clayton Baxter"), former Bush roommate at Andover and Yale

---

Because of his mother, George has always liked to surround himself with strong women. Condoleezza, Karen Hughes, of course. But you can trace it back as far as high school. I remember he dated this field hockey player who used to kick the shit out of him.

Alden Provost, Andover classmate

I'M PROBABLY THE ONLY GUY in our class who's actually lost weight since graduation. Eating goat'll do that to you. People ask what goat tastes like. I'd say it's still better than the meatloaf at the Yale cafeteria! [Laughs] As you can see, I haven't lost my turban-snapping humor.

MUHAMMAD AL-ZADR (NÉ "CLAYTON BAXTER"),
FORMER BUSH ROOMMATE AT ANDOVER AND YALE

When George got to Yale, he joined DKE, which was sort of the "jock fraternity." George wasn't an athlete, of course, but we had to let him in because his dad had been a member.

"SNAKE," FRATERNITY BROTHER

"HAD TO LET HIM IN because his dad had been a member." Noticing a pattern here? It's like *Single White Female* the way he copied my life.

GEORGE H. W. BUSH, FORMER PRESIDENT

We were hanging out in the DKE house the night of the moon landing. George had a massive bag of pot 'cuz he wanted to "be as high as the astronauts." He counted down, "Three—two—one—Ignition" and then lit up the bong. It was hilarious! But I gotta say it was also a little weird watching the guys hop around the moon while we were totally baked. I remember at one point George saying, "Dude, do you realize right now fifty percent of the moon's population is named 'Buzz'?" Some of the guys in the house were goofballs, but George was really deep.

"D-TRAIN," FRATERNITY BROTHER

While watching the astronauts hop around weightlessly, George pointed out, "That's how things used to be on earth before Isaac Newton discovered gravity."

"**Moosehead**," FRATERNITY BROTHER

Before George joined DKE, we'd do some hazing, but it was really primitive stuff. Whack a guy with a paddle. Make him go to the supermarket to get you a six-pack. That sort of thing. But then George arrived and brought it to a whole 'nother level.

"**Snake**," FRATERNITY BROTHER

George introduced a technique called "water boarding." The pledge is placed on an inclined board. Cellophane is spread over the pledge's face and the brothers then pour water on his face to simulate drowning. That was awesome! We were also the first fraternity to place electrodes on the pledge's penis. That was a tremendous breakthrough and it was all because of George.

"**D-Train**," FRATERNITY BROTHER

Years later when he first saw the torture photos from Abu Ghraib, President Bush got a big smile on his face. He said it was like looking at an old college yearbook.

John Ashcroft, FORMER ATTORNEY GENERAL

When I saw those torture photos, I immediately called George. We had a lot of laughs remembering old times. But you could also tell he was proud. I mean, here were some torture techniques we fooled around with when we were kids, being used by the most powerful military in the world! George compared it to a garage band suddenly having their songs played in Madison Square Garden.

"D-Train," FRATERNITY BROTHER

You have to realize, his entire life George had felt overshadowed by his father's achievements. His father was the better baseball player, the better student, and the war hero. But now, George had finally found something he was better than his father at—torturing people.

"Snake," FRATERNITY BROTHER

THE FIRST COUPLE YEARS GEORGE LOVED DKE, but by junior year he began to feel that one secretive, misogynistic organization wasn't enough. So he joined Skull and Bones.

"D-Train," FRATERNITY BROTHER

Like DKE, Skull and Bones was a group George's dad had been a member of. Again, George was let in as a legacy.

"Snake," FRATERNITY BROTHER

I MEAN, YOU'RE SEEING THIS, RIGHT?! Please tell me you're seeing this! Has the kid accomplished anything on his own?!

George H. W. Bush, FORMER PRESIDENT

Skull and Bones is shrouded in mystery. There are only a few details that are definitely known about it. For instance, one of the precepts of Skull and Bones is that if a nonmember ever says the words "Skull and Bones" in front of a member, the member has to immediately leave the room.

JEB BUSH, FORMER FLORIDA GOVERNOR

WE WERE WORRIED THAT BUSH WAS GOING to chicken out of going to war with Iraq. So whenever Bush started to raise questions during the war planning, Cheney would mutter "Skull and Bones" and George would have to leave the Situation Room. Oh my, George would get so pissed! We engineered an entire war and Bush wasn't around for any of it!

DONALD RUMSFELD, FORMER SECRETARY OF DEFENSE

Yes, I can confirm the incidents Secretary Rumsfeld has referred to. While President Bush believes the decision to send young men and women off to war *is* important, it is not nearly as important as maintaining the traditions of Skull and Bones. [Editor's note: At this point President Bush, who was standing next to Tony Snow, slumps his shoulders and reluctantly leaves the room.]

TONY SNOW, WHITE HOUSE PRESS SECRETARY

INTERVIEWER: Mr. Vice President, you claimed Iraq possessed weapons of mass destruction, which it didn't. You suggested there was a link between Iraq and 9/11, which there wasn't. You said our troops would be greeted as liberators, which they weren't. How can you justify being so cavalier with young men and women's lives?

CHENEY: Skull and Bones! [Cheney waits a moment and sees the interviewer isn't leaving the room.] Crap! Thought I might get lucky.

EXCERPT FROM CHENEY PRESS CONFERENCE MAY 19, 2006

CHAPTER 3

Vietnam: Those Who Got Cs in History Are Doomed to Repeat It

George really, really, really, really, really, really, really, really, really, really, really, really, really really, really, really, really didn't want to go to Vietnam.

BARBARA BUSH, FORMER FIRST LADY

YEAH, WHEN GEORGE SAID he didn't want to go off to war that surprised me, because he'd always been such a courageous guy, always willing to unselfishly sacrifice for the greater good. [Laughs sarcastically] I guess going off to war is the one part of my life he conveniently *didn't* want to copy.

GEORGE H. W. BUSH, FORMER PRESIDENT

I pleaded with my husband to find a way to get George out of the war.

BARBARA BUSH, FORMER FIRST LADY

I FIGURED WE SHOULD JUST SEND the Pentagon a photo of George in his cheerleading outfit and they'd classify him "Homo." But I took pity on the kid and broke out the checkbook.

GEORGE H. W. BUSH, FORMER PRESIDENT

For a guy who loves starting wars, George sure was a coward when it came to fighting 'em. You could balance the budget with the money his daddy spent helping him dodge the war.

LT. COL. MARK SPADA, FORMER MEMBER,
TEXAS AIR NATIONAL GUARD

GEORGE DID HIS TRAINING in Texas and then was sent to a base in Alabama. Well, at least that was the plan.

JEB BUSH, FORMER FLORIDA GOVERNOR

Hell, the United States had better luck tracking Osama than we did finding George when he was supposed to report for duty. Bush would disappear for months at a time. Then he'd show up wearing a "I Got Lei'd in Maui" T-shirt and saying some crap about how he was off "looking for weapons of mass destruction."

LT. COL. STEVE HOSTOMSKY, FORMER MEMBER,
992ND AIR RESERVE SQUADRON, MAXWELL AIR FORCE BASE, ALABAMA

I'M HIS OWN DAMN BROTHER and I don't know where George was when he was supposed to be in the National Guard.

JEB BUSH, FORMER FLORIDA GOVERNOR

Well wherever he was, when the war ended George felt it was safe to come home. So he moved back to Texas and essentially sat on his ass for fourteen years.

GEORGE H. W. BUSH, FORMER PRESIDENT

THIS COUNTRY HAS A PROUD TRADITION of self-made men who lift themselves up by their bootstraps. Abraham Lincoln teaching himself to read in front of the fireplace. Benjamin Franklin's mammoth lists of ways to better himself. So we were thrilled when President Bush was kind enough to donate his "Things to Do" list for 1977. When we opened it, however, we found there was only one entry for the entire year: "July 17—Eat a chili dog." His only plan for the entire year was to eat a chili dog on July 17?! Seriously, what does that even *mean*?

ROBERT BORDEN,
CURATOR OF GEORGE W. BUSH PRESIDENTIAL LIBRARY

I'll never forget the first time I saw George. A mutual friend hosted a barbeque and wanted us to meet. I immediately noticed his beautiful Armani slacks. Not only because they were so nice, but also because he was wearing them on his head.

LAURA BUSH, FIRST LADY

AT FIRST I HAD TROUBLE FIGURING OUT what George's appeal was for Laura. She had never dated a full-fledged alcoholic before, so I guess that was new.

NANCY AGOSTINI, FRIEND OF LAURA'S

On our first date George took me to a little honky-tonk bar outside of Houston. It was exciting for a girl who was used to spending all her time in the library to go to a bar. I had a piña colada. I even saved the umbrella from my drink. [Laura holds up a tiny umbrella from her scrapbook.] I also saved the umbrellas George got with his drinks. [Laura holds up approximately eighteen umbrellas.] He was such a gentleman. He very gallantly covered his mouth with a napkin when he threw up after his sixteenth piña colada.

LAURA BUSH, FIRST LADY

LAURA SAID ONE NICE THING about their first date was there wasn't that awkward "Will he kiss me?" moment at the end of the night. George got pulled over for DUI on the drive home. So they just had a lovely handshake as George was getting placed into the back of the squad car.

NANCY AGOSTINI, FRIEND OF LAURA'S

Three months after they met, they were married. That's how George acts. He trusts his gut.

JEB BUSH, FORMER FLORIDA GOVERNOR

I WASN'T INVITED, but I'm told it was a lovely ceremony.

MARVIN BUSH, BROTHER

He married a librarian. What a waste! A woman with access to all those wonderful books marries some bonehead who doesn't read. George W. Bush marrying a librarian is like me marrying a woman who works for Nike.

STEPHEN HAWKING, AUTHOR, *A BRIEF HISTORY OF TIME*

SHE'S NOT THE KIND OF WOMAN I'D MARRY. Laura always struck me as a wet rag. I'm betting she ain't exactly a hellcat in the sack. [Laughs] No wonder poor George has to experiment with hookers. [Playfully covers his mouth with his hand] Whoops, did I say that? Of course, who am I to talk? I've been screwing Mrs. Doubtfire for the last sixty years. Creeps me out the way that gray hair gets on my clothes. When we were dating, she looked normal. Turned out she'd been wearing a wig the whole time. On our wedding night she took it off, and I saw all that gray hair. [Shudders at the memory] I'm not gonna lie to you, I threw up all over her.

GEORGE H. W. BUSH, FORMER PRESIDENT

Every woman's dream—to offer yourself to your new husband and have him vomit on you like you're the president of Japan.

BARBARA BUSH, FORMER FIRST LADY

PRIME MINISTER.

GEORGE H. W. BUSH, FORMER PRESIDENT

In 1978 George was thirty-two years old and unemployed. The only thing he seemed to know how to do was BS with people and get drunk. That's all he did. Then one day he announced he was running for Congress. I was a little surprised at first, but then I realized it made sense. For a guy who just wanted to be a drunk, Congress actually seemed like a pretty good fit.

RICH KILLEEN, FRIEND

When George ran for Congress, he was a very inexperienced campaigner. Before his first speech, he put on a hammer and sickle pin his opponent had sent him for "luck." George put it on because he thought it looked cool.

Chris Schukei, 1978 CAMPAIGN MANAGER

He made a lot of "rookie" mistakes during the campaign. For instance, closing speeches by saying, "I believe America's best days are behind us!" I also felt vowing to relax child pornography laws was an odd issue to make the focus of your campaign. And going to a retirement community to propose "draconian cuts" in Medicare didn't help.

Hal Gurnee, CAMPAIGN POLLSTER

Rather than going around Texas trying to get votes, George decided to follow the Grateful Dead across the country instead. For ten months we drove around in his campaign bus smoking pot. He called it "grassroots campaigning."

Craig Finn, CAMPAIGN SPEECHWRITER

[Chuckling] Election day came and he got his ass handed to him. It was pretty satisfying.

George H. W. Bush, FORMER PRESIDENT

Even though he didn't put any work into it, George was really stunned when he lost. He thought winning elections was his birthright. But the loss taught him a valuable lesson for the next time he ran. He realized that instead of just sitting back and assuming you'll win, you really have to go out and put some effort into rigging an election.

Karen Hughes, LONGTIME STAFFER

After George failed at politics, he went crawling to Daddy begging for an oil company.

Jeb Bush, FORMER FLORIDA GOVERNOR

LET'S SEE—POLITICS, OIL. Check, check. Still ripping off the old man's life. You know, George often says that to understand him you must first understand Texas. But if you want to understand George, I recommend just reading a Richie Rich comic book; that'll pretty much tell you everything you need to know.

George H. W. Bush, FORMER PRESIDENT

George got some money from his father's buddies and started an oil company. He named the company "Arbusto," which is Spanish for "Bush." What George didn't realize is that "urbusto" means "jackass gringo pissing away Daddy's money." When George would walk by, the immigrants used to point at him and shout "Urbusto!" George would give them a big thumbs up. He thought they loved him.

Sheryl Zelikson, ARBUSTO SECRETARY

GEORGE DOESN'T LIKE to get bogged down in details; he goes with his gut. This was true even when he was in the oil business.

JAY JOHNSON, ARBUSTO VICE PRESIDENT

When it came to picking places to drill, George had no desire to read geological surveys or listen to the advice of experts. Instead he'd simply walk around Houston and let his gut tell him where the oil was. For instance, one day on the eighth hole of the Excalibur Country Club, George got a feeling there was oil. So we spent $11 million to buy the country club. We drilled for two years, but found nothing.

FRANK BYRD, ARBUSTO ENGINEER

ANOTHER TIME BUSH WAS DRINKING in a Houston bar called McGee's when his intuition kicked in. He insisted there was oil on that land, so we spent $3 million to buy the bar and surrounding property. Unfortunately, the land was dry. And so was the bar by the time George got through with it.

JAY JOHNSON, ARBUSTO VICE PRESIDENT

To his credit, there was one time when his intuition was right. George was walking along and suddenly froze. He said, "There's oil here! I can smell it!" Granted, he was standing in the middle of an Exxon station, but he was sort of right.

FRANK BYRD, ARBUSTO ENGINEER

CHAPTER 4

Just Your Typical Forty-Year-Old Slacker Sponging Off Mom and Dad

George was already feeling kind of self-conscious about his lack of accomplishments, and then in 1980 his dad was elected vice president.

BARBARA BUSH, FORMER FIRST LADY

THOUGH I DON'T AGREE with his politics, I feel a certain kinship with George W. Bush. We're both children of vice presidents. I can't speak for George, but I found that to be an amazing opportunity. You have direct access to one of the most powerful people in the world. You can use your influence to right wrongs, to change the world for the better. For instance, I urged my dad to cut the deficit.

KARENNA GORE SCHIFF, DAUGHTER OF AL GORE

I felt I helped influence U.S. policy by calling my father's attention to the ethnic cleansing in Kosovo, which was a cause I was very involved in.

Kristin Gore, DAUGHTER OF AL GORE

Sure, George tried to take advantage of the fact his dad was vice president. I remember he used to come into Friday's and threaten the owner that if he didn't get free potato skins, his daddy would shut us down.

Joanna DeMartin, FORMER T.G.I. FRIDAY'S WAITRESS

In 1981 George was still unemployed. With nothing else to do, he drove up to Yale to hang around the old fraternity house for a few weeks. I thought that was sort of weird for a thirty-five-year-old.

Laura Bush, FIRST LADY

He had this huge crush on Jodie Foster, who'd just enrolled at Yale. Talk about barking up the wrong tree. He'd sit outside the window of whatever class she was in and just stare at her.

Paula Chagares, JODIE FOSTER'S YALE ROOMMATE

I actually found George creepier than John Hinkley Jr., who was also lurking around me at the time.

Jodie Foster, FILMMAKER

GEORGE WAS SO JEALOUS when Hinkley shot Reagan for Jodie. George showed up at our dorm room that night and said, "Is that all it takes to impress you?! I'll shoot Daddy tomorrow, no problemo!" Jodie thought he was just talking, but then George actually tried to go through with it.

PAULA CHAGARES, JODIE FOSTER'S YALE ROOMMATE

[Smiling] Yeah, George tried to kill me to impress a woman who doesn't even like men. Brilliant. I rolled over in bed one night and there was George standing above me holding a gun. He accidentally had it pointed at himself, of course, so I wasn't real scared. Then he asked me where we kept the bullets. [Laughing] Bring it on, George.

GEORGE H. W. BUSH, FORMER PRESIDENT

JODIE DIDN'T WANT ANYTHING to do with George during college. She did call him years later, however, looking for Condoleezza's phone number.

PAULA CHAGARES, JODIE FOSTER'S YALE ROOMMATE

Yes, I knew about George's infatuation with Jodie Foster. That was a dark time. Our marriage was falling apart. George was drinking too much. We were constantly fighting. So we did what most couples do when they realize they're stuck in a failed marriage—have kids.

LAURA BUSH, FIRST LADY

Not only did I deliver George W. Bush, I also delivered his daughters. I'll never forget coming out of the delivery room and informing George he had twins. He got a very worried look on his face and asked, "Are they the stuck-together kind?"

Dr. Craig Thomas, OBGYN

Once we had children, I couldn't tolerate George's drinking any longer. I had a talk with him one night where I laid it on the line. I told George it was either the Jack Daniels or me. He said he chose me and threw out the Jack Daniels. The next day I came home to find him drinking a bottle of gin. Sometimes you really need to spell things out for George, almost the way you would with a "special" child.

Laura Bush, FIRST LADY

Hell, I'd drink too if I had to talk to Laura every night. [Imitating Laura] "Oh, I had such a crazy day at the library! A little boy returned *Charlotte's Web* and it was overdue, so I had to charge him a nickel. But he only had a dime, so I had to go into the back to get change!" I'd need at least a quart of gin to sit through that crap.

George H. W. Bush, FORMER PRESIDENT

I don't drink and George read somewhere that drinking alone means you're an alcoholic. So that's when he started giving beer to the dog. Apparently AA never thought to make "Drinking with the dog" a sign of alcoholism.

Laura Bush, FIRST LADY

If you drink beer with your dog, you might be an alcoholic.

UPDATED VERSION OF AA CHARTER

If you drink beer with your dog, you also might be a redneck.

JEFF FOXWORTHY, COMEDIAN

AS GEORGE APPROACHED FORTY, his dad said he wasn't going to support him anymore. George Sr. is very demanding. He felt if you're forty, you're old enough to have your own job.

LAURA BUSH, FIRST LADY

George was outraged that I was forcing him to get a job at forty. Called me an "ogre." Well, he tried to call me an "ogre," but he pronounced it "oougar."

GEORGE H. W. BUSH, FORMER PRESIDENT

GEORGE HAD NO DESIRE TO WORK. So if his dad wasn't going to support him, he decided to get his daughters to support him.

LAURA BUSH, FIRST LADY

It was crazy. I mean, we were three!

JENNA BUSH, DAUGHTER

ONE OF MY FIRST MEMORIES is Daddy coming into my room and throwing the classifieds at me.

BARBARA BUSH, DAUGHTER

Most of the civilized world has laws prohibiting three-year-olds from being put to work. So if you want your three-year-old to earn money, pretty much the only options you have are a Chinese sweatshop or the entertainment industry.

LAURA BUSH, FIRST LADY

SO WE WENT to Hollywood.

BARBARA BUSH, DAUGHTER

Hollywood is always looking for infant twins because they can play the same character and you get twice the work out of them.

JENNA BUSH, DAUGHTER

OF COURSE, playing the same person doesn't really work when one twin is a cute little girl and the other one is a fat slob.

BARBARA BUSH, DAUGHTER

Shut up, you anorexic bitch!

JENNA BUSH, DAUGHTER

THOSE GIRLS HAD SUCH beautiful smiles. I knew right away they were something special.

DAVID MINER, TALENT MANAGER

Things happened really quickly. We arrived on a Tuesday and had meetings set up for Wednesday.

BARBARA BUSH, DAUGHTER

I TOLD GEORGE that I set the girls up with an audition. He gave me a confused look and asked, "What's that?" I explained to him that it was sort of like a job interview. He gave me another confused look and asked, "What's that?"

DAVID MINER, TALENT MANAGER

We had an audition for *Full House,* but they ended up giving the role to the Olsen floozies. We probably would've gotten it, but Daddy ruined the audition.

BARBARA BUSH, DAUGHTER

WE WERE DOING A SCENE with Bob Saget when Daddy drunkenly stumbled onto the set. He tripped and fell face-first into a glass table. We did get $10,000 out of it when Saget showed the clip on *America's Funniest Home Videos.*

JENNA BUSH, DAUGHTER

Yeah, when George got to L.A. he really started partying hard. He fell in with a bad crowd.

ANDREA MAYWHORT, TALENT AGENT

THAT'S RIGHT! Bushie and I used to tear it up!

DAVID HASSELHOFF, FORMER WORKING ACTOR

Ironically, George was living in L.A. at the same time Dick Cheney was there playing Boss Hogg on *The Dukes of Hazzard.* They didn't meet, however.

CHRIS HARRIS, *THE DUKES OF HAZZARD* WRITER

HOLLYWOOD WAS FUN. But then Grandpa became president, so we came back home.

BARBARA BUSH, DAUGHTER

CHAPTER 5

A Time When the World Respected the Words "President Bush"

It's funny. Everybody loves to put George on the couch and look for Oedipal explanations for the decisions he makes. "He's invading Baghdad to do what his father couldn't do." "His dad hates Rumsfeld, so W. picks Rumsfeld to show up his father." Yet no one notices the things I used to do to piss off George. Why the hell do you think I picked Quayle as my vice president?!

George H. W. Bush, FORMER PRESIDENT

George was distraught when he found out about Quayle. He just sat there staring at the TV mumbling, "Apparently Daddy's found a frat boy/draft dodger he loves more than me."

Laura Bush, FIRST LADY

It was perfect. This Quayle yutz was now vice president of the United States while unemployed George was sitting home all day watching *Alf*. That was genius! It drove him crazy.

George H. W. Bush, FORMER PRESIDENT

I'LL ADMIT, "Dumb frat boy becomes vice president" is funny. I mean, it's the vice presidency. Even I couldn't screw that up. But "Dumb frat boy becomes president"? Dude, that's just scary.

Dan Quayle, FORMER VICE PRESIDENT

There was a real rivalry between Quayle and George W. It was similar to how Bobby Kennedy and LBJ used to vie for JFK's attention. Except imagine Bobby Kennedy and LBJ as a couple of idiots.

Colin Powell, FORMER SECRETARY OF STATE

WHEN QUAYLE MISSPELLED "potato," George was in heaven. He showed up at the White House the next day and started mercilessly mocking Vice President Quayle in a meeting.

Mary Barclay, FORMER ASSISTANT TO DAN QUAYLE

I finally said, "Okay, George. Why don't you tell us how to spell 'potato.'" That shut him up real quick. He starts mumbling, "I can't be expected to spell 'potato.' I'm not the vice president. I don't get the classified memos he does. Blah, blah, blah." So then I said, "Okay, how 'bout 'shovel'? You figured out how to spell that one yet?" George turned red and mumbled, "I gotta go clear some brush." That's his excuse whenever he wants to get out of something: "I gotta go clear brush." Yeah, like there's a lot of brush in downtown D.C.

George H. W. Bush, FORMER PRESIDENT

BRUSH? The only thing he cleared out was the liquor cabinet.

LAURA BUSH, FIRST LADY

Yeah, around that time George's drinking was out of control. During a trip to Colorado, he finally hit rock bottom. I take that back. He hit what I *thought* was rock bottom, until he discovered even new lows with Iraq and Katrina. Anyway, I asked the Reverend Billy Graham to meet with George and give him some guidance.

GEORGE H. W. BUSH, FORMER PRESIDENT

I TOOK GEORGE FOR A WALK and began telling him about God. I timed it so that right as I got to my big finish, we turned the corner to find the *Knight Rider* car sitting in the middle of the street. I got Mr. T to record a message as KITT saying, "I'm God and I pity the fool who don't believe in me!" Well, George completely bought it. He fell to the ground sobbing. He knelt before KITT's zigzagging red light and begged, "You can take Laura and the kids—just please don't hurt me!"

REV. BILLY GRAHAM, RELIGIOUS DUDE

Years later, President Bush invited me to the White House to discuss Iraq. At one point I used the phrase, "I pity the fool"—I believe I was discussing beleaguered Iraq foreign minister Hoshyar Zebari. Anyway, when I said it, President Bush looked at me and said, "I appreciate the Biblical allusion."

MR. T, ACTOR/STATESMAN

George loves baseball. It's the one constant running through his entire life. Well, that and Asian hookers. [Playfully covers his mouth] Whoops, did I say that?!

George H. W. Bush, former president

It's testimony to President Bush's ability to recognize the issues that are important to the average American that even with all the trouble in the Middle East, he still insisted on devoting a portion of the 2004 State of the Union to the problem of steroids plaguing baseball. He's disgusted by steroid users who take what he calls a "shortcut to success." President Bush believes success should come only as a result of hard work—or family connections.

Michael Gerson, former White House speechwriter

George W. Bush owned the Texas Rangers when they had Jose Canseco, Sammy Sosa, Pudge Rodriguez, and Rafael Palmeiro on the team. Yet Bush couldn't find any steroids in the locker room. And we're supposed to be surprised he didn't find any weapons of mass destruction in Iraq?

Peter Gammons, Hall of Fame sportswriter

George spent $600,000 to buy a piece of the Rangers and then later sold his share for $14 million. How did he make over a $13 million profit? He bet like crazy against the Rangers!

Pete Rose, gambling great

As far as the gambling accusation, I'll admit Mr. Bush occasionally asked us to make some questionable moves. For instance, one night he ordered Nolan Ryan to pitch underhanded. Another time Mr. Bush picked a random fan to be our centerfielder for the night. It just so happened the fan he picked was an eighty-five-year-old woman with a new hip.

Bobby Valentine, FORMER RANGERS MANAGER

Yes, the artificial hip definitely limited my mobility in the field. But then in the ninth inning, Canseco stuck a needle in my ass and I cranked the game-winning home run.

Stephanie Birkitt, EIGHTY-FIVE-YEAR-OLD FAN

Sure, looking back it's obvious Bush was throwing games. But with George your initial reaction is that he's just a dumbass. I honestly thought it was stupidity, not greed.

Fay Vincent, FORMER BASEBALL COMMISSIONER

Judging by the way he's been running the country, I wouldn't be surprised to learn he's been betting against the United States.

Bobby Valentine, FORMER RANGERS MANAGER

CHAPTER 7

Before Schwarzenegger. Before Jesse "The Body." The Original Embarrassing Governor

Owning the Rangers made him famous in Texas. He then was able to use that fame to get elected governor.

LAURA BUSH, FIRST LADY

THE BUSH FAMILY was so excited about George becoming governor. When I mentioned the limousine had arrived to take George to the governor's mansion, his mom said, "Mansion? Cool, do we get slaves?!"

MELISSA KEARNEY, FORMER BUSH ADVISER

As far as what type of leader he chose to model himself after, Bush has always felt a certain kinship with Kim Jong Il.

KAREN HUGHES, LONGTIME STAFFER

YEAH, WE BOTH HAD powerful fathers who wanted us to get involved in politics. And there are many issues of leadership that we bonded over—the right of a ruler to spy on his own citizens, the importance of surrounding yourself with lackeys who'll help you live in denial, the right of a leader to view himself as above the law.

KIM JONG IL, NORTH KOREAN LEADER

When Bush became governor, he decided to appoint a "director of propaganda," which is an idea he got straight from Kim Jong.

KAREN HUGHES, LONGTIME STAFFER

MY ROLE WAS TO GIVE the citizens the leader they wanted. I hesitate to use the term "brainwashing," because that phrase has such a negative connotation. But really, what's wrong with brainwashing? What's wrong with administering a cleansing of the population's brain? We began with a direct-mailing campaign to let the people know more about George W. Bush.

KARL ROVE, DIRECTOR OF PROPAGANDA

Governor Bush played golf for the first time this morning. He shot a 26 with ten holes in one! How blessed we are to have one kissed by God as our governor!

EXCERPT FROM A 1995 DIRECT-MAILING FLYER
SENT OUT BY GOVERNOR BUSH

ALL HAIL GOVERNOR BUSH who took the form of Troy Aikman earlier today to lead our Dallas Cowboys to a Super Bowl victory! Governor Bush then bedded the hot chick that appeared in the Doritos Super Bowl commercial!

EXCERPT FROM 1996 DIRECT-MAILING FLYER

Our governor, who is angry about the meager donations citizens are making to his reelection campaign, created the tornado that ravaged Galveston yesterday. We must send more money to appease him, lest our governor make the sun disappear and the moon turn to blood.

EXCERPT FROM 1998 DIRECT-MAILING FLYER SENT BY GOVERNOR BUSH

WHEN HE BECAME GOVERNOR, George tried to officially change the state's name to "Tex-ass." That was an issue he really cared about. And he also got a big kick out of executing people.

KAREN HUGHES, LONGTIME STAFFER

We did a photo op where then-Governor Bush had his picture taken with Koko, the gorilla who can sign one thousand words. There were a couple embarrassing moments when Koko used words that the governor didn't know. But George W. Bush has such a curious mind, he went home and looked up the words in the dictionary. I'll never forget how proud he was later that day when he used the word "hibernation" correctly in a sentence.

KARL ROVE, DIRECTOR OF PROPAGANDA

The governor always liked to let off some steam before the weekend. So we'd have margaritas and karaoke in the office every Wednesday afternoon. We did it on Wednesday, because Thursday and Friday were kind of "blow off" days for the Governor.

Dan Fetter, ASSISTANT TO GOVERNOR BUSH

After a few years as governor, Dad wanted something more. So in 1999 he told my sister and me that he wanted to run for president. But he said that we were his number one concern. Dad assured us that he wouldn't run if we didn't want him to. Well, we hated the idea of giving up our privacy, so we told him we didn't want him to run. The next day he announced his candidacy.

Barbara Bush, DAUGHTER

He looked us right in the eye and lied to us. That's the moment when I first realized, "Wow, he really *could* be president."

Jenna Bush, DAUGHTER

The key to George W. Bush's presidential appeal was that he was an outsider. He wasn't one of those career politicians who's a creature of Washington. People really responded to the fact that George W. Bush was a regular guy with no connection to D.C. I mean, aside from the fact that his daddy was vice president for eight years. Or that his daddy was also president. Or that his grandfather was a U.S. senator. But besides that, he's a total outsider. No connection to Washington.

Matthew Dowd, REPUBLICAN POLLSTER

As the campaign began, we were worried that the liberal media might focus on George's alcoholism and past drug use. We wanted to avoid George's drinking and remind voters that the election was all about character.

Karen Hughes, longtime staffer

Everyone had heard the rumors about George's past, so we decided that on the campaign trail he'd answer all those questions by repeating the line, "When I was young and irresponsible, I was young and irresponsible." It worked pretty well. Before arriving at that line, however, we did road test a few others that didn't work as well:

- "When I was young and addicted to cocaine, I was young and addicted to cocaine."
- "I think the most honest thing to say is that I *am* an alcoholic. It's an ongoing struggle that you never fully defeat. And should I get a job as stressful as the presidency, it carries with it the very real possibility of relapse."
- "I haven't snorted blow in nearly two years."

Karl Rove, director of propaganda

Reporter: Governor Bush, have you ever used cocaine?

Bush: I'm not interested in rehashing the past. I'm focusing all of my energy on dealing with the tough issues facing this country. Now if you'll excuse me, I have a photo op with the zoo's new panda.

George W. Bush,
campaigning before the 2000 New Hampshire primary

Bush defeated me in the South Carolina primary by spreading rumors that I was insane and that I'd fathered a black baby. After the primary, then-Governor Bush gave a victory speech in which he thanked me for "bringing out the best" in him. And I remember thinking, "Oh my God! That was him at his *best*?!"

John McCain, U.S. SENATOR

OBVIOUSLY, THE DECISION of who would be vice president was enormously important. Ideally you want to "balance" the ticket. So if you have a southerner at the top of the ticket, you want a northerner for vice president. Or if you have a young presidential candidate, you balance the ticket with a more experienced vice president. In the case of George W. Bush, we were hoping to balance the ticket by finding a vice president who was smart, hard working, and capable.

Dan Bartlett,
COUNSELOR TO THE PRESIDENT, CHIEF OF COMMUNICATIONS

Dick Cheney was placed in charge of the vice presidential search committee. Cheney made up a list of what qualities we should look for in a vice president—someone who had been a secretary of defense, someone who had been CEO of an oil conglomerate, someone bald, someone overweight with a bad heart, and, ideally, someone with a lesbian daughter. Okay, in hindsight his criteria may have been a tad self-serving.

Andy Card, FORMER CHIEF OF STAFF

I REALIZE IT MIGHT APPEAR suspicious that Cheney ended up as the vice president. In his defense, however, when you consider his charisma, his good looks, his integrity, and the three electoral votes Wyoming held—well, Dick Cheney really was the best candidate for the job.

KAREN HUGHES, LONGTIME STAFFER

We were all worried about Cheney's heart condition. Before offering the position, we invited him down to Austin to discuss his medical status over dinner. So what did Cheney order at this dinner concerning his fragile heart? A sixty-four-ounce steak! I'm telling you, Cheney's swallowed more meat than any politician this side of James McGreevey.

DAN BARTLETT,
COUNSELOR TO THE PRESIDENT, CHIEF OF COMMUNICATIONS

THE INITIAL MEETING BETWEEN Bush and Cheney was a little awkward. Then-Governor Bush kept complimenting Cheney on how good his English was. Bush then began lightly touching Cheney's scalp while asking, "How did they remove that purple spot?" Well, it turned out Bush thought he was talking to Mikhail Gorbachev.

KAREN HUGHES, LONGTIME STAFFER

That's the first time anybody's ever mistaken me for a Commie, I can tell you that much.

DICK CHENEY, VICE PRESIDENT

[Editor's note: Dick Cheney actually joined the Communist Party in 1968 as part of his increasingly desperate attempt to avoid military service in Vietnam. Mr. Cheney was a member of the Communist Party until 1975. To his credit, by all accounts Mr. Cheney served the Communist Party with honor.]

SO CHENEY JOINED the ticket and then came the controversy of the 2000 election.

ANDY CARD, FORMER CHIEF OF STAFF

Look, we can sit here and discuss the Florida recount and what illegal things we may or may not have done. But I have something that might take your mind off those nosey questions.

KARL ROVE, DIRECTOR OF PROPAGANDA

[Editor's note: At this point, Rove snaps his fingers and Karen Hughes enters wearing a XXX-L dungaree negligee. She begins mannishly stroking my hair. Horrified, I forget about the recount and hurry out of the room.]

CHAPTER 8

Economy's Good, There's a Budget Surplus, America's at Peace . . . Yeah, the Country Needs a New Direction

Good God.

GEORGE H. W. BUSH'S COMMENT TO FRIENDS AFTER HIS SON WAS DECLARED PRESIDENT

THE MORNING OF BUSH'S inauguration, we invited George and Laura up to the residence for coffee. As you might expect, it was a slightly awkward situation. For instance, it was hard to hear the conversation over Bill's sobbing. Laura tried to break the tension by making a little small talk. She asked me which detergent works best for getting DNA out of clothing. What a stupid bitch.

SEN. HILLARY CLINTON, FORMER FIRST LADY

When George stood in front of Justice Rehnquist to take the oath of office, he saw the black robe and out of habit immediately pled "Guilty" to drunken driving.

Jeb Bush, FORMER FLORIDA GOVERNOR

HEY, REHNQUIST, rip off a piece of that Bible so I can ditch my Hubba Bubba.

FIRST OFFICIAL WORDS OF THE BUSH PRESIDENCY,
JANUARY 20, 2001, 12:01 P.M.

During the inauguration, somebody told George he was the forty-third president and that I was the forty-first. Well, the next day George had these hats made up: "43" and "41." He gave me the hat and stood there like he was all proud of himself. You know, like he'd just split the atom or something. I had to put the hat on because there were a lot of photographers around, but it was pretty gay if you ask me.

George H. W. Bush, FORMER PRESIDENT

FORMER PRESIDENT BUSH would like to apologize to any homosexuals offended by the derogatory term he used while describing a hat given to him by his son. The former president wants to assure the gay community that he harbors no ill will toward homosexuals. In fact, former President Bush believes the odds are he probably hired some homosexuals to work in the White House, albeit unwittingly.

STATEMENT FROM **Jaime Becker,**
SPOKESWOMAN FOR GEORGE H. W. BUSH

The most embarrassing moment of my life came at one of the inaugural balls in 2000. I was dancing with Daddy when the strap on my dress broke. It started to fall down right in front of everybody! All those photographers were standing there; you may have seen the photo of me trying to hold my dress up. I just wanted to crawl into a hole!

JENNA BUSH, DAUGHTER

THAT STORY MIGHT BE CUTE if it was the first time Jenna's top just "magically" popped off. It's hard to think of a place Jenna's top *hasn't* come off—frat parties, bars, Mr. Mulligan's English class, the waiting room at Jiffy Lube, church, in front of every guy I've ever had a crush on. [Barbara stares at the photo of Jenna's dress mishap at the inaugural.] They say a picture's worth a thousand words, but I'm honestly having trouble coming up with 999 words other than "whore."

BARBARA BUSH, DAUGHTER

George is a real student of history. The first day of his presidency, he just strolled around the White House soaking it all in. He was asking a million questions like "When does the money come out with me on it?" "Am I allowed to eat a bald eagle?" "Who's the loser who has to work in that stupid round office?"

KARL ROVE, DIRECTOR OF PROPAGANDA

A FEW DAYS AFTER he took office, I came to Washington to brief the president about a possible smallpox pandemic. I gave him the various contingency plans the CDC had prepared in the event a strain of smallpox fell into the hands of terrorists. President Bush didn't seem to be paying much attention to my presentation, however. He was more concerned with the kung fu magazine he was reading. When I finished, the only question Bush asked was, "Hey, are albinos contagious?"

JEREMY WEINER,
CENTERS FOR DISEASE CONTROL AND PREVENTION

Because he's not a Washington insider, President Bush isn't beholden to typical Washington thinking. He's able to "think outside the box," as we say in Texas. I remember soon after he took office we had a freewheeling discussion on ways to counter global warming. While the stuffed shirts were talking about lowering emissions, President Bush was the one issuing the bold new ideas—invading Antarctica, pouring Gatorade on the sun, fast-tracking construction of an eighty-story air conditioner in Nebraska to cool the country.

KAREN HUGHES, LONGTIME STAFFER

IN ADDITION TO GLOBAL WARMING, we were also very interested in putting the kibosh on stem cell research and evolution.

ANDY CARD, FORMER CHIEF OF STAFF

Some of our stances have created this misconception that President Bush is somehow antiscience. Nothing could be further from the truth. The president believes in *sound* science. And by sound science, he means things that have been tested. Not newfangled notions like evolution, which we've barely had a century to study.

ARI FLEISCHER, FORMER WHITE HOUSE PRESS SECRETARY

I WAS CAPTAIN OF MY college baseball team; he was a male cheerleader. I was a war hero; he was a draft dodger. I was a respected world leader; he's a buffoon. Is it any wonder the nitwit doesn't believe in evolution? That's right, don't tread on me, bitch!

GEORGE H. W. BUSH, FORMER PRESIDENT

Yes, we discussed global warming and evolution in the early days, but honestly that wasn't our top priority when we took office. You really don't get much healthy food on the campaign trail. As a result, President Bush gained about five pounds during the 2000 campaign. So getting "ripped" was the central issue on his mind at the start of his presidency.

KAREN HUGHES, LONGTIME STAFFER

THE FIRST ONE HUNDRED DAYS, President Bush focused primarily on cardio like running and bicycling to lose the weight. After that, his attention turned to abs and glutes. Six months into his presidency, Bush was technically two pounds heavier than when he took office, but that's because muscle is heavier than fat. He was looking good.

KARL ROVE, DIRECTOR OF PROPAGANDA

I work out a lot. Bicycle. Weights. Not to brag, but I know if it ever came to it, I could kick the ass of any other president. That provides me with a great source of comfort during times of trouble. I could beat up Jefferson, Eisenhower, FDR. Well, not FDR. I'd never beat up a gimp. Unless, you know, he had it coming. Like if he bumped into me or something. In addition to Nautilus, I've also learned some kung fu. So let's say Jimmy Carter came at me with a knife. I'd use a little monkey claw on him—rip his eye out of its socket before he even knew what hit him.

GEORGE W. BUSH STATEMENT AT PRESIDENTIAL COUNCIL ON FITNESS EVENT

THE FIRST FEW MONTHS of his presidency, everything was clicking. President Bush's body fat index was down 36 percent from where Bill Clinton's was at a comparable time in his presidency. Blood pressure, muscle mass, all the indicators were where you wanted them to be. But then, of course, President Bush's carefully orchestrated workout schedule was thrown into upheaval by the devastating attacks of September 11th.

KAREN HUGHES, LONGTIME STAFFER

September 11th. I'll never forget that awful Thursday morning. [Editor's note: Tuesday.]

DICK CHENEY, VICE PRESIDENT

PRESIDENT BUSH WAS READING "The Pet Goat" to our class. I remember the chief of staff entered and whispered something in President Bush's ear. Then Bush screamed, "Oh my God! America's under attack! We're all gonna die!" A bunch of us kids had to calm him down.

BILLY NORRETT, STUDENT AT EMMA E. BOOKER ELEMENTARY SCHOOL

The Secret Service begged me to go down into the bunker, but I refused. I felt at that moment, *especially* at that moment, America needed to see me, their president [Editor's note: Vice] standing tall in the face of terror. [Editor's note: Vice President Cheney did in fact go to the underground bunker as numerous White House photos prove.]

DICK CHENEY, VICE PRESIDENT

I FINALLY GAVE THE PRESIDENT my juice box. I figured if he was drinking juice at least he wouldn't be screaming, "We're all gonna die!"

BILLY NORRETT,
STUDENT AT EMMA E. BOOKER ELEMENTARY SCHOOL

I immediately knew that this was the work of Saddam, which history has proven, I might add. [Editor's note: It really hasn't.] Furthermore, I knew that . . . [Cheney takes a sip of water and then stands up.] Do you mind if we take a five-minute break? The heart attacks are starting to come closer together.

DICK CHENEY, VICE PRESIDENT

IT TOOK PRESIDENT BUSH a day or two to find his footing after September 11th. The image of him nervously flying from Florida to Louisiana to Nebraska in the hours after the attack didn't inspire much confidence. And then he wasn't at his best when he addressed the nation from the Oval Office that night.

ANDY CARD, FORMER CHIEF OF STAFF

Well, he began the Oval Office address by screaming "Dammit, Superman, where are you?! Save us, Superman!" Thankfully, we had him on a ten-second delay, so the nation didn't see that.

Michael Gerson, FORMER WHITE HOUSE SPEECHWRITER

We knew we had to come up with a powerful image to "change the story." We needed to project Bush as a strong leader. So September 12th we had an emergency meeting of the communications team. It was myself, Gerson, and Dan Bartlett. We were just brainstorming and that's when we came up with the idea.

Karl Rove, DIRECTOR OF PROPAGANDA

Karl was making us laugh by "burping" the national anthem. He curled up a piece of paper to amplify the sound. And that's when it hit me—a bullhorn!

Dan Bartlett, COUNSELOR TO THE PRESIDENT, CHIEF OF COMMUNICATIONS

We decided to send Bush to Ground Zero with a bullhorn. We paid a construction worker in the crowd to shout out "We can't hear you." Bush's scripted reply was, "I can hear you. The rest of the world hears you. And the people who knocked down these buildings will hear all of us soon!" I still get goose bumps. It's the most important thing I'll ever write.

Michael Gerson, FORMER WHITE HOUSE SPEECHWRITER

I'm still amazed it never got out that we faked it. I mean, wasn't anyone suspicious that they never saw the construction worker who said, "We can't hear you"? Wasn't anyone suspicious that we live in an age of media, yet we never saw a profile on this guy? Wouldn't you expect to see him on *Oprah* and *Larry King* and the *Today* show? Wouldn't you expect him to write a book called *He Heard Me* or perhaps a self-help book titled *Make Yourself Heard*? Well that didn't happen because as soon as he said the line, we made him disappear so he couldn't squeal. [Chuckles] Yup, we sent him off to the same place the Chinese sent the Tiananmen Square dude who stood in front of the tanks.

Dan Bartlett,
COUNSELOR TO THE PRESIDENT, CHIEF OF COMMUNICATIONS

Well, there are no more elections, so I guess it's safe to talk about now. Yes, of course, we faked it. "I can hear you. The people who knocked down these buildings will hear all of us soon." Honestly, does that sound like the kind of thing George W. Bush would come up with on the spot? We've been watching him stumble around for seven years. Do you really think that in the ruins of Ground Zero he suddenly ad-libbed a pitch-perfect line for the first time in his life? Of course not. We faked it! But fortunately for us, people believe what they want to believe. So the people believed.

Karl Rove, DIRECTOR OF PROPAGANDA

In the days after 9/11, the White House pressured the EPA to delete some of the scarier parts from our report on the air quality around Ground Zero. I now realize the cover-up resulted in many workers developing respiratory problems. As an attempt to make amends, I'd like to publicize the phrases that were originally deleted from the report:

- "The air is highly toxic."
- "This situation is extremely dangerous."
- "Workers must evacuate immediately."
- "The air is almost as bad as Jersey's."

Christie Todd Whitman, FORMER EPA HEAD

After America was attacked, President Bush realized it was imperative that he reach out to other foreign leaders to build a global coalition. [Editor's note: He did?] Fortunately for our country, there's no one better than President Bush at mastering those one-on-one relationships. The other world leaders all like and respect him.

Ari Fleischer, FORMER WHITE HOUSE PRESS SECRETARY

The first time I met President Bush, he asked me to thank the French people for giving America the Grand Canyon as a gift. When I told him I believed he was thinking of the Statue of Liberty, he glared at me and said, "Don't tell me about my country, Froggie!" I remember thinking he was a, well, I believe the American word is "numbskull."

Jacques Chirac, PRESIDENT OF FRANCE

Whereas diplomacy often gets lost in a sea of translations and policy papers, President Bush excels in forging a *human* connection with other leaders. That's where the nicknames come in, which even the president's harshest critics would have to admit he's a master of.

Ari Fleischer, FORMER WHITE HOUSE PRESS SECRETARY

The first time I met President Bush, he looked exhausted. I asked if he was jet-lagged. He told me, "No, I was up all night trying to think of a good nickname for you." I asked him what he came up with and he told me, "Danza.' You know, Tony like Tony Danza." I recall thinking, "The world could be in a spot of trouble."

Tony Blair, BRITISH PRIME MINISTER

HE TOLD ME MY NICKNAME was "Rubik's Cube," because he says I was big in the '80s. I was so pissed off, I "accidentally" sold some plutonium to North Korea.

COL. MUAMMAR QADDAFI, LIBYAN LEADER

CHAPTER 9

Bush and Rove: The Two Men You Want Planning Your War

[Editor's note: In hindsight, the State of the Union address President Bush gave on January 28, 2003, stands as one of the most important moments of his presidency. It was in this speech that Bush laid out the case for going to war with Iraq. To accomplish this, he relied on the since-debunked report that Saddam Hussein attempted to purchase uranium from Africa. How did the flawed piece of intelligence about yellowcake from Niger make it into such a monumental speech? We have acquired the e-mails Karl Rove sent to Bush in the days leading up to the speech, which cast a fascinating new light on the inner workings of the Bush presidency.]

To: G. W. Bush
From: Karl Rove
Re: Your idea

Mr. President, your proposal is interesting. While there's nothing in the "Constitution" specifically prohibiting us from turning the State of the Union into a fund-raiser, it may look a tad greedy. I'm afraid you may have to "suck it up" and make this one a freebie.

To: G. W. Bush
From: Karl Rove
Re: Your joke

I agree that opening with a joke can be a nice icebreaker, but as far as the one you're considering–I must remind you that a significant number of midgets vote. [I know, I know–I'll put that on the list of things to address in the second term.]

To: G. W. Bush
From: Karl Rove
Re: Midgets voting

I actually don't know how they reach the levers. Phone books? I'll give Stephanopoulos a call. :)

To: G. W. Bush
From: Karl Rove
Re: Your query

Uhh, I haven't really given it much thought, but I guess I'd say Godzilla would beat up King Kong.

To: G. W. Bush
From: Karl Rove
Re: Your query

Well, Godzilla can shoot that laser-y fire stuff out of his mouth for starters, but I really think we need to focus on the speech, Mr. President.

To: G. W. Bush
From: Karl Rove
Re: Swinging for the fences

We need a big *moment* in the speech a la JFK challenging America to put a man on the moon.**To:** G. W. Bush
From: Karl Rove
Re: Swinging for the fences

Yes, sir, you have told me how "baked" you were the day of the moon landing. Great story, sir. Anyway, I suggest we propose a bold new initiative in which we give an 80 percent tax cut to all registered Republicans! This is just the kind of "red meat" our base is looking for and will send a "get with the winning team" message to swing voters.

To: G. W. Bush
From: Karl Rove
Re: Niger

We received a tip that Saddam attempted to buy some yellowcake in Niger. If true, Saddam could use a bomb to create instability in the region and affect the world's oil supply. Even worse, if Saddam sells it to a more technologically advanced enemy, the yellowcake could be used to level an American city. Mr. President, I can't stress the gravity of this threat enough—yellowcake could potentially kill tens of thousands of Americans.

To: G. W. Bush
From: Karl Rove
Re: Yellowcake

Yes sir, you did sound just like Homer Simpson when you said "Mmmm, yellowcake."

To: G. W. Bush
From: Karl Rove
Re: Niger

I urge you to practice saying "Niger" a few more times before the speech. A mispronunciation like the one you made yesterday in the Oval would be catastrophic.

To: G. W. Bush
From: Karl Rove
Re: Reaching out

Interesting. I agree that if you mispronounce "Niger" we'll need to reach out to inner-city voters, but I worry that ripping open your shirt to reveal a "Thug Life" tattoo could end up being a "Dukakis in the tank" moment for us.

To: G. W. Bush
From: Karl Rove
Re: Yellowcake

Okay, just got word the Saddam yellowcake rumor is bogus. But I think it still makes for a good story, so I say we run with it. What's the harm?

To: G. W. Bush
From: Karl Rove
Re: Link to Paris Hilton video

Dude, the speech can wait. You gotta check this out!!!!

The great thing about President Bush is he didn't need to spend hours reading through documents concerning the yellowcake reports. His gut told him it sounded right and that's all he needed to decisively march to war.

Karl Rove, DIRECTOR OF PROPAGANDA

For all the criticism of Bush's performance, his achievements are actually pretty impressive when you consider he's only working two and a half hours a day. Sure, Lincoln may have accomplished more, but that's not a fair comparison, because he was working eighteen-hour days.

Karen Hughes, LONGTIME STAFFER

I chuckle at liberals who complain President Bush doesn't work hard. He doesn't *need* to work as hard as most people. He's blessed with supernatural intuition. It was his intuition that told him Dick Cheney was the right choice for vice president. It was his intuition that told him Donald Rumsfeld would be an amazing secretary of defense.

Douglas Feith,
FORMER UNDERSECRETARY OF DEFENSE FOR POLICY

President Bush trusts his gut. His gut told him invading Iraq was the right thing to do. So he was able to make his decision without getting bogged down by CIA reports questioning the existence of WMDs. He was unencumbered by briefing papers on what postwar reconstruction of Iraq would entail or boring Pentagon papers speculating on numbers of casualties.

Paul Wolfowitz,
FORMER DEPUTY SECRETARY OF DEFENSE

I'm so sick of hearing all this shit about Bush's "gut" and his amazing intuition. Who is he—freakin' Miss Cleo?! His powers of perception are no better than any other person's. It's just an excuse to get out of doing things he doesn't want to do, like reading or thinking. But he's got a famous name, so his whole life nobody's called him on it.

George H. W. Bush, FORMER PRESIDENT

CHAPTER 10

Mission Accomp . . . Hey, What the Hell Happened?!

Obviously working at the White House is a very demanding job, but there are some fantastic perks. For instance, the boys at Halliburton sent everybody fruit baskets to thank us the day after we started the war with Iraq.

JOSH BOLTEN, CHIEF OF STAFF

SOON AFTER THE WAR BEGAN, we received a tip that Saddam Hussein was eating lunch at the al-Sa'ah, a restaurant in the Baghdad suburb of Mansur. We dropped four bombs from a B1 Lancer and destroyed the restaurant. But unfortunately it turned out Saddam wasn't there.

GEORGE TENET, FORMER HEAD OF CIA

We later learned the tip had been called in by the manager of the local Applebee's. It seems he was just trying to get rid of the competition.

GEN. GEORGE W. CASEY, ARMY CHIEF OF STAFF

IN MY DEFENSE, the Applebee's manager sounded super-duper sure Saddam was there.

GEORGE TENET, FORMER HEAD OF CIA

A week later we got a tip that Saddam was hiding in a Baghdad school, so we blew up the school early one morning.

GEN. GEORGE W. CASEY, ARMY CHIEF OF STAFF

YEAH, TURNS OUT THAT TIP was called in by a young Iraqi boy who was just trying to get out of trigonometry. It seems he had a quiz that day. In hindsight, perhaps I should've known the phone call wasn't credible based on all the giggling.

GEORGE TENET, FORMER HEAD OF CIA

Then we obtained a tip that Saddam was hiding in a Range Rover parked outside a bar in Georgetown, so we blew that up. The car, however, turned out to belong to the president's daughter Barbara.

GEN. GEORGE W. CASEY, ARMY CHIEF OF STAFF

[LAUGHING] Yeah, I called that one in. I was seriously P.O.'d because Daddy bought Barbara a Range Rover for her birthday, but forgot my birthday. How do you forget it's also my birthday? We're twins!

JENNA BUSH, DAUGHTER

Sure, a lot of the tips we received turned out to be wrong. And obviously our credibility took an enormous hit when we went into Iraq and didn't find any weapons of mass destruction. To all the families who lost loved ones, I offer a heartfelt "Whoops."

PAUL WOLFOWITZ, FORMER DEPUTY SECRETARY OF DEFENSE

MANY AMERICANS, of course, turned on the war when no weapons of mass destruction were found. I once asked President Bush if he ever considered planting WMDs in Iraq after the invasion. He gave me a look of regret and sadly muttered, "Sure, *now* you tell me."

TOM BROKAW, FORMER NBC ANCHOR

We'd been riding high for so long, but then in early 2004 things started to turn against us. The Richard Clarke book, a Bob Woodward book, and the Paul O'Neill hatchet job all came out around the same time and were just devastating. We decided to go on the offensive and make books the enemy.

ARI FLEISCHER, FORMER WHITE HOUSE PRESS SECRETARY

BASICALLY, EDUCATED PEOPLE are more likely to vote Democrat, so we wanted to try and, I don't wanna say "stamp out" reading, but curtail it to some degree.

KARL ROVE, DIRECTOR OF PROPAGANDA

We had Laura Bush give a speech in which she challenged kids to watch twelve hours of TV a day. Being a former librarian gave her the moral authority to tell kids not to read. It was a real "Nixon goes to China" moment for her.

ANDY CARD, FORMER WHITE HOUSE CHIEF OF STAFF

It never really took off, but we experimented with a pilot program in Gary, Indiana, called "Books for Guns." If a kid traded in a book, we'd give him a gun.

Karl Rove, DIRECTOR OF PROPAGANDA

The president went so far as to give a speech on the South Lawn flanked by NBA stars/dropouts like Carmelo Anthony in which he proposed giving $25,000 to every college student who dropped out.

Rod Paige, FORMER SECRETARY OF EDUCATION

"Imagine a world in which thousands of young men and women escape the suffocating shackles of parental expectations and break out of the imprisoning classroom to pursue the freedom of starting rock bands, joining the NBA, or just sitting around playing video games." That's a line I'm particularly proud of.

Michael Gerson, FORMER WHITE HOUSE SPEECHWRITER

Yes, our poll numbers started to crater in 2004, but the president is very good about keeping morale up. No matter what's going on in the world, he wants everybody out of the office by 3:30 p.m., 3:45 tops. And when he senses people are down, he'll lighten the mood by making a joke about Katrina or doing an impression of Michael J. Fox.

Josh Bolten, CHIEF OF STAFF

To help get the nation "psyched," sometimes in lieu of a speech President Bush will use his Saturday radio address to give the nation an Aerosmith "twofer."

Dan Bartlett, COUNSELOR TO THE PRESIDENT, CHIEF OF COMMUNICATIONS

To make work more fun, he also started an office pool in which you won $1,000 if Cheney had a heart attack on your birthday.

Josh Bolten, CHIEF OF STAFF

In addition to the bad news out of Iraq, the economy was also struggling. Bush claimed it was a high priority to him, but I always felt that if he was really serious about giving our economy a boost, he would've ordered his daughters to switch to domestic beer.

Alan Greenspan, FORMER CHAIRMAN OF THE FEDERAL RESERVE

The president showed up to our first economic meeting with a couple baseball mitts. He asked me a bunch of questions about what Derek Jeter was like. Obviously he thought he'd hired the baseball player Paul O'Neill. I did my best to keep up the charade, but I wasn't entirely convincing.

Paul O'Neill, FORMER SECRETARY OF THE TREASURY

Yeah, at one point the ball hit him in the shin and he started crying. That started to make the president suspicious.

Andy Card, FORMER CHIEF OF STAFF

President Bush finally told me to either stop "throwing like a girl" or I'd be out of a job. The next day Andy Card informed me I was being sent down to Johnny Bench's baseball instructional camp in Florida to work on "fundamentals." I spent the bulk of my time as treasury secretary shagging fungos and taking BP. I was honestly so busy learning how to hit a curveball that I didn't notice we'd racked up the biggest deficit in history.

PAUL O'NEILL, FORMER SECRETARY OF THE TREASURY

PRIOR TO THE 2004 ELECTION, we toyed with the idea of President Bush stepping down to focus on campaigning. We had an election to win and didn't want him getting sidetracked by the annoying details of the presidency.

KARL ROVE, DIRECTOR OF PROPAGANDA

Some feared stepping down might make the president look like a quitter, but we were prepared to explain to the American people that there is a proud history of presidents who left office before their term was complete—Lincoln, Kennedy, Nixon.

SCOTT MCCLELLAN, FORMER WHITE HOUSE PRESS SECRETARY

ONE OF THE STUMBLING BLOCKS was we couldn't agree on an appropriate buyout package for the president to receive from the American people. Bush wanted a deal commensurate with the $36 million windfall Dick Cheney received when he stepped down from Halliburton. So ultimately it was decided that President Bush would remain president.

KARL ROVE, DIRECTOR OF PROPAGANDA

I honestly didn't want to go through another campaign in 2004. There's simply too much mudslinging and nastiness.

LAURA BUSH, FIRST LADY

YEAH, IT GOT A LITTLE ROUGH in '04. For instance, the Kerry camp accused President Bush of being scared to debate. That's ridiculous. George W. Bush never runs away from a fight—except for Vietnam, of course.

SCOTT MCCLELLAN, FORMER WHITE HOUSE PRESS SECRETARY

When Kerry got the nomination, I won't lie to you—we were worried. Well, I *would* lie to you, but I'm actually not lying right now.

KARL ROVE, DIRECTOR OF PROPAGANDA

KERRY WAS A VIETNAM HERO and Bush wasn't. Rather than avoiding the subject, however, we decided to make Vietnam a central issue in the campaign. It's all part of Karl Rove's political jujitsu—take your enemy's strength and make it a weakness. How do you do that? You make shit up!

DAN BARTLETT, COUNSELOR TO THE PRESIDENT, CHIEF OF COMMUNICATIONS

We got the "Swift Boat Veterans for Truth" guys to run some commercials that cast doubt on Kerry's war record. The liberal media was angry because we were distorting the facts, but it worked.

KAREN HUGHES, LONGTIME STAFFER

PEOPLE SAY I SHOULD order the "Swift Boat" veterans to stop running these commercials attacking Kerry. Well, I can't control what commercials come on TV. Look, there are a lot of commercials out there that I wish I could get rid of. For instance, how 'bout that Cialis ad where it looks like the old coots are gonna do it? I mean that's just gross.

PRESIDENT BUSH
DURING 2004 INTERVIEW WITH CNN'S WOLF BLITZER

Hey, don't knock Cialis. That stuff's a miracle worker.

WOLF BLITZER'S RESPONSE TO PRESIDENT BUSH

THE "SWIFT BOAT" lies worked so well, we pushed it even further. President Bush called a press conference in which he held up a dented Purple Heart and told the nation that he was also a Vietnam hero.

KARL ROVE, DIRECTOR OF PROPAGANDA

The dented Purple Heart was actually one of Kerry's that he threw away when he was protesting the war in the '70s. Bush happened to have been at the antiwar rally and picked it up.

DAN BARTLETT,
COUNSELOR TO THE PRESIDENT, CHIEF OF COMMUNICATIONS

YEAH, PRESIDENT BUSH used to go to a lot of antiwar demonstrations in the '70s because he said the hippie chicks were really easy.

KARL ROVE, DIRECTOR OF PROPAGANDA

After Bush held up the medal, Kerry was so angry. He called us up and screamed, "That's my medal!" [Laughs] Hey, finders keepers, Rambo.

DAN BARTLETT,
COUNSELOR TO THE PRESIDENT, CHIEF OF COMMUNICATIONS

WE FELT WE COULD DISTORT Kerry's Vietnam record, but our big concern was Kerry getting another war hero on the ticket. I was constantly e-mailing President Bush as we prepared for Kerry to announce his running mate.

KARL ROVE, DIRECTOR OF PROPAGANDA

To: G. W. Bush
From: Karl Rove
Re: Kerry V.P.

Not everyone screws up their V.P. pick like you and Daddy (LOL), so we need to be ready in the event Kerry picks a war hero like John McCain or Wesley Clark.

To: G. W. Bush
From: Karl Rove
Re: Clark

Yes, "Wesley" is his real name, but no, I don't think he's gay.

We could've withstood Wesley Clark, but if McCain had joined Kerry's team there's no way we would've recovered. And Kerry was pressuring McCain hard. Kerry even got that nut-job ketchup wife of his to offer McCain a brand-new Camaro if he joined the ticket.

KARL ROVE, DIRECTOR OF PROPAGANDA

I'VE ALWAYS WANTED a Camaro and the one he offered me was pretty sweet. It was cherry red. Tell me I wouldn't have gotten laid cruising around in that thing cranking a little Def Leppard. But I told Kerry, "I'm a United States senator. I can't be bribed." I misspoke, of course. What I meant to say was, "*Despite* the fact I'm a United States senator, I can't be bribed."

JOHN MCCAIN, U.S. SENATOR

We lucked out when McCain didn't join Kerry, but to win we still needed our base out to come out in force. So we made stem cells an issue.

KARL ROVE, DIRECTOR OF PROPAGANDA

THE PRESIDENT IS A VERY MORAL MAN. Ethics are at the center of every decision he makes. That's why he vetoed further stem cell research, because he doesn't believe taxpayers' money should go toward something they find morally objectionable. Well, aside from the Iraq War, of course.

SCOTT MCCLELLAN, WHITE HOUSE PRESS SECRETARY

To appease the Christian conservatives we also pushed for the Constitutional amendment banning gay marriage.

KARL ROVE, DIRECTOR OF PROPAGANDA

I REMEMBER WHERE I WAS when I heard the news about the amendment—I was in a Detroit motel hooking up with a Hooters waitress.

MARY CHENEY, LESBIAN DAUGHTER

I THINK THE GAY MARRIAGE ISSUE caused some friction between Vice President Cheney and his daughter. During the campaign you could see it was getting to him. Cheney wasn't his usual happy-go-lucky self. I remember one day he screamed at me that the lighting we were using for his speeches made him look fat and bald. Yeah Dick, it's the lights.

ANDREW EVANGELISTA, LIGHTING DIRECTOR, 2004 CAMPAIGN

A lot of people ask how I could end up a lesbian after growing up in a Republican household. Well, consider the male role model I was exposed to during my formative years. If you'd grown up around my dad, you'd be turned off men, too.

MARY CHENEY, LESBIAN DAUGHTER

As the campaign came down to the final days, we were looking for any edge to help us win. So a week before the election we put out a commercial saying, "To ensure things are more organized than the chaotic 2000 election, this year we're dividing Election Day into two days. If you plan to vote for Bush, go to the polls Tuesday, November 2. To vote for John Kerry, go to the polls Thursday, November 4." [Laughs] The idiots in Ohio really bought it.

KARL ROVE, DIRECTOR OF PROPAGANDA

IT WAS A GOOD THING WE RIGGED OHIO, because the election was even closer than we were anticipating. Some of our key supporters didn't end up voting for us.

MATTHEW DOWD, REPUBLICAN POLLSTER

Daddy was seriously ticked when he found out I voted for Kerry. (Stupid wiretaps!) Well, maybe he should've gotten me the Range Rover.

JENNA BUSH, DAUGHTER

CHAPTER 11

Letting New Orleans Get Washed Away and a Couple Other Minor Bloopers

The day after he was reelected, George started calling me "Mr. One Termer." I never forgot that. I let him spew his cocky crap. And all the while I sat there silently plotting my revenge. Silently plotting like a ninja. The ninja my government trained me to be when I fought the Japs. Then in 2005 the wheels came off his presidency, and I knew it was my time to strike. After Katrina, I replaced George's gay little "43" hat with a "29%" hat in honor of his approval rating. When he saw it, I thought he was gonna cry. I'll say it again—don't tread on me, bitch!

George H. W. Bush, former president

There's that famous photo of President Bush flying over the wreckage done by Katrina. Many saw that image as an example of Bush being disengaged, but I recall him being very interested. I'll never forget the way he looked out the window and said, "Wow, what happened down there?"

Andy Card, former chief of staff

He seemed very upset when we flew over New Orleans, so to cheer him up we quickly put *Austin Powers* on as the in-flight movie. The liberal media loves to complain about how slow the government was to respond to the effects of Katrina, but we had that DVD on in less than thirty seconds.

Scott McClellan, FORMER WHITE HOUSE PRESS SECRETARY

BUSH HAS INSTRUCTED the staff that he never wants to be "sad." I'm proud to say *Austin Powers* worked and when we got back to D.C. it was like the hurricane never happened.

Andy Card, FORMER CHIEF OF STAFF

People criticize the government for not responding, but in our defense, we had no idea the media was going to keep reporting on the aftermath of Katrina. I mean, the press never bothered to assess blame for 9/11, and they basically ignored the lack of WMDs in Iraq, so we figured they'd let this slide as well. I swear to you, had we known that we were going to take the PR hit we did, we would've dealt with Katrina the day it happened.

Karl Rove, DIRECTOR OF PROPAGANDA

NEARLY A WEEK AFTER the hurricane, President Bush finally came to Louisiana. He and I took a helicopter tour to observe the devastation of New Orleans. I'll never forget, the president pointed down to the flooding and said, "How cool would it be if all that was beer?!" And then for the first time in my life, I found myself high-fiving a president.

Ray Nagin, NEW ORLEANS MAYOR

[Editor's note: Besieged with attacks for his mishandling of Katrina, President Bush attempts to turn the page by telling reporters, "There will be a time to take a step back and to take a sober look at what went right and what went wrong."]

I was incredibly proud of the president for making that statement. President Bush made it clear he didn't want the focus to be on who was to blame for Katrina. He selflessly took the spotlight off himself to try and put it on the people who had suffered. That's real leadership.

Karl Rove, DIRECTOR OF PROPAGANDA

After President Bush declared that blame would be assessed at a later date, there were a lot of questions as to when exactly that would be. We decided on February 18, 2094. So feel free to give us a call then with all of your Hurricane Katrina complaints.

Andy Card, FORMER CHIEF OF STAFF

With everyone criticizing us about the hurricane, we were relieved when William Rehnquist went terminal because it allowed us to "change the story" by picking a new Supreme Court justice. President Bush did a great deal of research and picked the smartest, finest legal mind in the land—Ms. [twenty-five-second pause] you know, the chick with the raccoon eyes. [Editor's note: Harriet Miers.]

Dick Cheney, VICE PRESIDENT

PEOPLE IMMEDIATELY ATTACKED the choice just because Miers had never actually been a judge. That was really an absurd criticism. I mean, that's like saying someone shouldn't be a pilot just because they've never been on an airplane before.

KARL ROVE, DIRECTOR OF PROPAGANDA

You sort of got the feeling Miers wasn't ready for prime time. When she walked into the courtroom for a photo op, she pointed to the gavel on the bench and asked, "Wow! Is Gallagher coming?!"

DAVID SOUTER, SUPREME COURT JUSTICE

I LIKED HER. When Scalia walked by, Miers pretended to cough and said, "Rogaine!"

STEPHEN BREYER, SUPREME COURT JUSTICE

I noticed that whenever we asked her a question about the law, she would pretend to drop something and then sneak a look at a Magic 8 Ball she had in her purse.

ARLEN SPECTER, MEMBER OF THE SENATE JUDICIARY COMMITTEE

IN ADDITION TO BEING TERRIBLY UNQUALIFIED, Harriet Miers looked ridiculous. The raccoon eyes, the tacky bright blue outfits. So in an attempt to salvage her nomination, the White House image team gave Miers a makeover. They got rid of the black eyeliner. They put her in more conservative colors. She actually started looking pretty good.

DAN BARTLETT,
COUNSELOR TO THE PRESIDENT, CHIEF OF COMMUNICATIONS

Damn straight she started looking good! Miers was looking F-I-N-E fine! I dreamed of placing my left hand on her judicial body and letting my fingers go to work like a naughty stenographer. I still fantasize about dragging her down into my underground lair, where I would hold her—not in contempt—but in passion as the two of us made a sex tape that would shock even Clarence Thomas!

JOHN ASHCROFT, FORMER ATTORNEY GENERAL

[FORMER PRESIDENT BUSH ENTERS and immediately makes a face as if detecting a strange aroma.] By the smell of it in here, I'm guessing you just finished an interview with Ashcroft. God, did he take a *bath* in gin?

GEORGE H. W. BUSH, FORMER PRESIDENT

Everyone was talking about how hot Miers looked after the makeover. So I pulled her aside, held a nail file to her throat, and informed her, "*I'm* the hot babe on this Court! You got that, bitch?! My booty is slammin', hussy!" She withdrew her nomination later that day. They replaced her with that fine hunk of man Sam Alito, who quickly made me his little "boy toy."

RUTH BADER GINSBURG, SUPREME COURT JUSTICE

[Editor's note: On September 14, 2005, during a meeting of the U.N. Security Council, a camera caught President Bush writing a note to Condoleezza Rice that read, "I may need a bathroom break? Is this possible?" We asked Condoleezza Rice about the incident.]

[Laughs] Yes, the president drank a little too much Yoo-hoo prior to the meeting. He needed that Yoo-hoo sugar rush to reduce the chances of falling asleep during the discussion about Iraq. Thankfully we never have to worry about Vice President Cheney needing a bathroom break, because he wears adult diapers.

Condoleezza Rice, secretary of state

Part of the secretary of state's job is dealing with those little notes President Bush hands you throughout the day. Here are a few I saved over the years

- July 17, 2002: "Hey Powell, I ate too many Fritos! Stomach hurts!!!!"
- November 12, 2003: "Hey G.I. Joe, can I please, please, please have a turtle?"
- May 19, 2004: "Hey E. Coli, I think I accidentally left the nuclear codes at Blockbuster."

Colin Powell, former secretary of state

CHAPTER 12

Road Trip!

Admittedly President Bush didn't travel much overseas before he took office, but he really does an amazing job representing our country in foreign lands.

Karl Rove, DIRECTOR OF PROPAGANDA

In 2003 President Bush came to England for a state visit. He seemed to enjoy being here. He told me that driving on the left side of the road reminded him of his drinking days.

Tony Blair, BRITISH PRIME MINISTER

When he travels overseas, President Bush wants to learn everything he can about the local culture. I recall once while we were in Mexico, we overheard some villagers chanting and the president asked, "What does the phrase 'Yankee imperialist dog' mean in English?"

Condoleezza Rice, SECRETARY OF STATE

In Latin America I overheard him saying, "What a coincidence. That dummy being burned in effigy looks just like me."

Colin Powell, former Secretary of State

In 2005, Mexico hosted a North American summit in Cancun. President Bush said the last time he'd been to Cancun was when he had to bail his daughters out of prison.

Vicente Fox, former Mexican President

Yeah, we went to Cancun for 2002 Spring Break. We were partying at Señor Frogs when I had a fight with the stupid dago bartender. [Editor's note: Not a "dago," the Mexican bartender was a, well, Mexican.] He gave me a margarita with salt. I specifically ordered a margarita without salt. Salt retains water. If I have salt, I'll blow up like Jenna. So I threw my glass through the front window. Jenna and I had to spend the night in a Mexican prison.

Barbara Bush, daughter

I couldn't believe it—the prison was full of Mexicans! The conditions were awful. One hundred and thirteen women and only three showers. I was like, "What is this—Vassar?!"

Jenna Bush, daughter

I'm probably not one to criticize a parent for letting their kid become an alcoholic, but seriously, those girls are a mess.

George H. W. Bush, former President

Whenever I meet with President Bush, he thanks Mexico for being the United States' "proud neighbor to the north." And I'm supposed to stand there and act deferential to him?!

VICENTE FOX, FORMER MEXICAN PRESIDENT

ONE THING THAT STRUCK ME during the summit I hosted in Russia, instead of "Hail to the Chief" President Bush entered to a song called "Bad to the Bone." Because he entered to a different song than what my thugs were expecting, it totally threw off our plan to poison him with polonium-210.

VLADIMIR PUTIN, RUSSIAN PRESIDENT

Yes, entering to "Bad to the Bone" was President Bush's idea. The president actually gets many of his ideas from pro wrestling.

CONDOLEEZZA RICE, SECRETARY OF STATE

THANKSGIVING 2004 President Bush stunned the world with his surprise visit to Iraq. It was a tightly guarded secret. In fact, to protect the surprise and avoid leaks we didn't even inform the president beforehand.

ANDY CARD, FORMER CHIEF OF STAFF

As we approached the Baghdad airport, President Bush looked out the window and said, "Wait, this doesn't look like Crawford. Where the hell are you taking me?" He was so scared.

TOM CATUSI, SECRET SERVICE AGENT

ACTUALLY, THE ONLY PERSON in the world who knew about the Iraqi visit was the Air Force One pilot. I didn't know. Cheney didn't know. Bush didn't know. Just the pilot. It was his idea. I guess you could technically call it a "kidnapping."

ANDY CARD, FORMER CHIEF OF STAFF

Hey, it was my last week before retiring. I decided to have a little fun.

MATT ROBERTSON, FORMER AIR FORCE ONE PILOT

THE VISIT TO IRAQ was pretty good, but I always thought if President Bush *really* wanted to surprise people, he should've visited the Oval Office once in awhile.

ANDY CARD, FORMER CHIEF OF STAFF

When flying into Iraq, the pilot has to make a rapid descent while engaging in what's called a "corkscrew landing" to avoid drawing enemy fire. It's the same evasive move that we have to use to avoid gunfire when landing at Cheney's place.

MATT ROBERTSON, FORMER AIR FORCE ONE PILOT

IN 2006 PRESIDENT BUSH made his second visit to Iraq. Again, to maintain the surprise, the details were closely guarded. Only a few people knew about it. All of the reporters were herded onto buses in D.C. and told they were being taken to Camp David. It was only later that they found out they were in fact going to Iraq. I guess it's nice that Bush went over to visit the troops, but it tells you something about the guy that even when he does something good, he has to lie about it.

Colin Powell, FORMER SECRETARY OF STATE

On the flight over to Iraq I spent a lot of time trying to give the president an understanding of the tension between the Sunnis and the Shiites. After I spent about five hours explaining it to him, he looked at me and said, "So they're sorta like the Yankees and the Red Sox." Yes! It felt so good to really get through to him.

Condoleezza Rice, SECRETARY OF STATE

During one of our visits to Baghdad, an Iraqi villager approached the president. He said, "If Iraqis steal, they get a hand cut off. How do you still have two hands after what you pulled in the 2000 election?" [Chuckles] President Bush asked to torture that guy personally.

Terry Murray, SPECIAL ASSISTANT TO THE PRESIDENT

A great many of the Iraqi people were under the impression that George W. Bush was a popular American comedian, because they'd seen the hilarious movie *Fahrenheit 9/11*.

Nouri al-Maliki, IRAQ PRIME MINISTER

When giving a speech, it's always good to open with a joke. So for his speech in Iraq, I gave President Bush the line, "I'm pleased to announce that Iraq is well on its way to a stable democracy." That got a big laugh.

Michael Gerson, FORMER WHITE HOUSE SPEECHWRITER

The Iraqi government was a mess. When they informed us they couldn't meet the deadline to write the country's constitution, President Bush snapped, "Why don't you do what I did at Yale? Just get a pledge to write it for you!"

Paul Bremer, FORMER PRESIDENTIAL ENVOY TO IRAQ

People think President Bush spends all of his time on Iraq. Iraq only takes up about an hour, which leaves another forty-five minutes of the workday to focus on other areas of the world. The president is concerned with many different countries. For instance, in 2006 he made a visit to India.

Andy Card, FORMER CHIEF OF STAFF

We gave him some briefing books to prepare for the trip. Bush opened one of them, saw a photo of Gandhi, and asked, "Hey, when did Osama lose the beard?" Suffice to say, I cancelled my dinner reservations for that night.

Condoleezza Rice, SECRETARY OF STATE

Yeah, Condi cancelled because she had to tutor the nitwit on India. I was disappointed, because I had a lovely night planned—tickets to see Melissa Etheridge and then we were going back to my place to watch some *Xena* DVDs.

Mary Cheney, LESBIAN DAUGHTER

I know everybody thinks Condi's a lesbian. And I'll admit, she's got a hell of a lot of Indigo Girls songs on her iPod. But I still think there's something going on between her and George. [Chuckles] Hey, it's not like I've never been with a black woman. Do you remember the hoochie who played Aunt Esther on *Sanford and Son*? We used to get very, very busy. Anyway, forgive my interruption. Please get back to your stories about [feigning a yawn] India.

George H. W. Bush, former president

The international Air Force One flights were always a lot of fun. I remember on the flight to India, Bush drank twenty-two beers, which broke Rosalynn Carter's Air Force One record.

John Ashcroft, former attorney general

Yeah, I was on that flight. I don't recall Bush drinking twenty-two beers, but I do remember thinking, "Hmm, Condi and the stewardess sure seem to be hitting it off."

Donald Rumsfeld, former secretary of defense

When the president arrived in India, he stepped off the plane and gave me a bear hug. He said, "How's it hanging PB and J?" I still don't understand why he calls me "PB and J."

A. P. J. Abdul Kalam, president of India

The president read some of Gandhi's writings while we were over there. After finishing one essay espousing nonviolence, President Bush closed the book and mumbled, "Pussy."

Condoleezza Rice, secretary of state

THE ENTIRE TIME we were in India, Bush kept asking where the Indian casinos were. He even brought $40 in quarters hoping to hit the slots.

RANDI GROSSACK, U.S. ENVOY TO INDIA

When he couldn't find any Indian casinos, he started patting his hand to his mouth while imitating a Native American war cry. The president said this was his way of "smokin' out the Injuns."

ANDY CARD, FORMER CHIEF OF STAFF

WE TOOK PRESIDENT BUSH to a ceremonial meditation session. When the guru told the president to empty his mind, Andy Card muttered, "He's way ahead of you."

A. P. J. ABDUL KALAM, PRESIDENT OF INDIA

For six years I held my tongue on all my "Bush is an idiot" jokes, but that one slipped out.

ANDY CARD, FORMER CHIEF OF STAFF

ANDY MADE THE JOKE. Five minutes later I was the new White House Chief of Staff.

JOSH BOLTEN, CHIEF OF STAFF

We spent one day at Vishakhapatnam. After the first speech we were ninety minutes behind schedule as a result of President Bush trying to pronounce "Vishakhapatnam."

MICHAEL GERSON, FORMER WHITE HOUSE SPEECHWRITER

WE TRIED TO MAKE THINGS easier for the President by just referring to Vishakhapatnam as 'Nam, but as soon as he heard the word "'Nam," Bush climbed up a tree and refused to come down.

CONDOLEEZZA RICE, SECRETARY OF STATE

When I told President Bush that our population was over a billion people, he looked at me and said, "God, how much did it cost to rig *your* election?!" I was insulted, but not surprised. The president said a number of insulting things during his trip.

A. P. J. ABDUL KALAM, PRESIDENT OF INDIA

MY NAME IS SHRI BHAIRON SINGH SHEKHAWAT. That is the name my father chose for me. I did not appreciate President Bush referring to me as "Injun Joe."

SHRI BHAIRON SINGH SHEKHAWAT, VICE PRESIDENT OF INDIA

CHAPTER 13

Daddy Becomes Friends with Clinton: A Disturbing Early Sign of Dementia?

Iraq was really the final straw in George Sr. and George W.'s relationship. When the war took a turn for the worse, they stopped speaking.

BARBARA BUSH, FORMER FIRST LADY

YEAH, THAT'S TRUE. The war severed our relationship. So at least some good has come from it.

GEORGE H. W. BUSH, FORMER PRESIDENT

Don't let the wimp fool you. The estrangement from George W. kills him. When George stopped calling, you could see George Sr. getting depressed. He was just puttering around the house with nothing to do. And I couldn't spend much time with him because I was busy attending my Klan meetings.

BARBARA BUSH, FORMER FIRST LADY

Oh yeah, Babs never misses a rally.

Michael Richards, actor

That's why George's friendship with former President Clinton was such a blessing. It gave him something to do, and as an added bonus, it made George W. insanely jealous.

Barbara Bush, former first lady

George came up to visit Kennebunkport one weekend, and I "forgot" to warn him that I had invited President Clinton to come up as well. I gave George's old room to Clinton. [Throws his head back and laughs] Oh, it was priceless. George was stomping around the house like a jealous thirteen-year-old girl.

George H. W. Bush, former president

I was all over Laura that weekend and Bush didn't seem to care. But whenever he saw me talking to the old man, he'd flip out.

Bill Clinton, former president

At one point former President Clinton and I were trying to have a discussion about reshaping the Middle East, you know, just president-to-president. Well, George—excuse me [Smirking and making exaggerated air quotes with his fingers] "Forty-three" kept bothering us and asking if he could help. So I tossed him a pair of his old cheerleading pom-poms and said, "Here, make yourself useful."

George H. W. Bush, former president

It was pretty damn funny.

Bill Clinton, FORMER PRESIDENT

Everybody was surprised to see Dad and Clinton become friends. The media dubbed them "The Odd Couple." But in reality there was nothing odd about it—Dad wanted to make George jealous and Clinton was trying to ingratiate himself into the family so he could hit on the Bush daughters.

Jeb Bush, FORMER FLORIDA GOVERNOR

President Clinton was obviously interested in the idea of "scoring" with twins. That's something only a handful of presidents have accomplished. Kennedy, of course, Warren Harding, and, surprisingly, Jimmy Carter. [Editor's note: Officials at the Jimmy Carter Presidential Library confirm that Carter hooked up with the "Doublemint Twins" in 1978.] So Clinton saw this as an achievement that could finally cement his legacy. There's no question Bubba went to Kennebunkport hoping to get his freak on.

Arthur Schlesinger Jr., PRESIDENTIAL HISTORIAN

I had the biggest crush on Clinton when I was in high school. I even kept a photo of him from his grand jury testimony hanging in my locker. And Jenna knew I liked him. So, of course, the first time we met him, her blouse was dropping to the floor faster than Daddy's approval rating.

Barbara Bush, DAUGHTER

Hey, maybe my blouse falling was an accident, maybe it wasn't. The point is at least I *had* something to show him, unlike my flat-chested sister.

Jenna Bush, DAUGHTER

CLINTON MADE DADDY FEEL like the most important guy in the world. But it was clearly all an act. We just didn't want to see Daddy get hurt.

Jeb Bush, FORMER FLORIDA GOVERNOR

He got sort of pathetic around Clinton. Every day it was "I wonder if Bill wants to play horseshoes." "I wonder if Bill wants to see a movie." "I wonder if Bill will like me in this shirt."

Barbara Bush, FORMER FIRST LADY

CLINTON, MEANWHILE, wasn't exactly subtle about his motives. Dad planned a humanitarian trip for the two of them in Africa. Clinton says, "Hey, I bet the twins would love to see a tour of the genocide in Darfur! Let's invite 'em along!"

Jeb Bush, FORMER FLORIDA GOVERNOR

The day they were supposed to leave for Darfur, George came home from the mall with a T-shirt he made for Bill. It had a photo of the two of them and it read "Friends 4-ever!" That's when I knew he was gonna get hurt.

Barbara Bush, FORMER FIRST LADY

Two hours before they were supposed to leave, Jenna and Barbara suddenly announced they didn't want to go.

Jeb Bush, FORMER FLORIDA GOVERNOR

I was drunk when I originally agreed to go. Hell, I'll say "Yes" to anything when I'm drunk, as anyone who's seen that women's prison movie I made in Mexico will attest. [Editor's note: The film, *Not Innocent II: Cancun*, is certainly worth renting.]

Jenna Bush, DAUGHTER

So when the twins bailed, Clinton looks at Dad and says, "Well, I ain't going if it's just me and the coot." Poor Dad was so upset he started throwing up.

Jeb Bush, FORMER FLORIDA GOVERNOR

Grandpa was vomiting like Nicole Richie after a trip to Dairy Queen.

Jenna Bush, DAUGHTER

Hey, Jenna, maybe you should try purging once in awhile.

Nicole Richie, "CELEBRITY"

I thought Bill was going to Africa, but then he came home five days earlier than he was supposed to, which was a little awkward. He walked in on Antonio Banderas and me taking a bath.

Sen. Hillary Clinton, FORMER FIRST LADY

SHE TOLD ME THEY WERE DISCUSSING NAFTA, which I knew was a load of crap because it's the exact same excuse I told her when she caught me playing nude Twister with Penelope Cruz.

BILL CLINTON, FORMER U.S. PRESIDENT

CHAPTER 14

Mission Accomp . . . Wait, We *Still* Haven't Won This Thing?!

As the situation in Iraq worsened, the army began having trouble meeting its recruitment goals.

DONALD RUMSFELD, FORMER SECRETARY OF DEFENSE

AT FIRST WE CONSIDERED reinstating the draft. We thought we'd start by drafting people born on April 23 like, oh I dunno, Michael Moore. And then people born August 17 like, well let's see, Sean Penn.

PAUL WOLFOWITZ, FORMER DEPUTY SECRETARY OF DEFENSE

One day Cheney was reading an article about how popular those Civil War reenactments are. So he got an idea.

DONALD RUMSFELD, FORMER SECRETARY OF DEFENSE

THE U.S. ARMY invites you to take part in a 1991 Gulf War Reenactment! That's right, for only $1,200 we'll provide you with the once-in-a-lifetime chance to act like a real-live Gulf War soldier! We'll fly you to Iraq! We'll give you a gun! And best of all, we'll let you shoot at Iraqis—just like in the real Gulf War!

EXCERPT FROM CHENEY'S U.S. ARMY RECRUITMENT COMMERCIAL

About 2,500 idiots signed up. [Chuckling] I'll tell you, ol' Dick earned his $22 million a year with that one!

DONALD RUMSFELD, FORMER SECRETARY OF DEFENSE

GIVEN ALL THE PROBLEMS with Iraq, most people expected Donald Rumsfeld to offer his resignation in 2004. Look, Cheney and Rummy didn't give up their cushy multimillion-dollar jobs in the private sector to make a measly $200,000 working for the government. They each have enormous bonuses buried in the federal budget. But if Rummy quit, he didn't get squat. So he was trying to get fired for three years before Bush finally pulled the trigger; Bush really didn't want to see him get the money.

ANDY CARD, FORMER CHIEF OF STAFF

As Iraq descended into chaos in 2005, it was an extremely frustrating time for me. I mean, I honestly didn't know what else I could do to get fired. I tried everything short of taking a leak on the Oval Office carpet. [Editor's note: A frustrated Rumsfeld finally *did* take a leak on the Oval Office carpet on July 17, 2006.]

DONALD RUMSFELD, FORMER SECRETARY OF DEFENSE

I HAVEN'T SEEN STAINS like that on the Oval Office rug since the Clinton years.

VINNIE FAVALE, WHITE HOUSE CUSTODIAN

With so much focus being paid to Iraq, at home America remained woefully unprepared for another terrorist attack. There were still gaping holes in our defense. For instance, in May 2005 a small plane accidentally entered White House airspace. The military was terribly slow in scrambling jets to intercept it.

TOM KEAN, COCHAIR, 9/11 COMMISSION

WE DID ARREST THE PILOTS when they landed. President Bush was riding his bicycle in Maryland at the time, so he wasn't in any danger. We questioned the pilots to see if it was a potential terrorist attack, but they assured us, "If we were trying to get President Bush, we know the last place he'd be in the middle of the day is at work."

MICHAEL CHERTOFF, HOMELAND SECURITY SECRETARY

Curbing terrorism requires remaking the entire Middle East, so in 2006 we invited Palestinian President Mahmoud Abbas to the White House for some diplomacy.

CONDOLEEZZA RICE, SECRETARY OF STATE

President Bush kept peppering Abbas with questions about "Dancing Queen." He was also dropping hints that he wanted free tickets to *Mamma Mia.* When we explained to President Bush that he was speaking to the leader of Palestine, not a member of ABBA, he looked at his watch and said, "Wow, 3:30 p.m. Quittin' time!" and blew out of the room.

Stephen Hadley, NATIONAL SECURITY ADVISER

To try to make President Bush think the war was going okay, we used to show him footage from the first Gulf War. It worked pretty well until one day we didn't stop the tape in time and the president asked, "Why is Daddy addressing the nation from the Oval Office?"

Paul Wolfowitz, FORMER DEPUTY SECRETARY OF DEFENSE

We realized that sometimes the president can appear stubborn, so in 2006 we finally got him to concede that some mistakes had been made in Iraq. The public responded to his honesty and his poll numbers jumped up slightly. Well, thinking he'd stumbled on a winning formula, the next day the president gave a speech in which he reminded the American people that he was also the dumbass behind the high gas prices, the mammoth debt, the worsening of the environment, and Katrina.

Matthew Dowd, REPUBLICAN POLLSTER

One thing President Bush had no intention of apologizing for was the wiretapping program he started. At one point Senator Arlen Specter threatened an investigation into our spying on the

American people's phone calls. Ol' Arlen sort of backed off his threats once we informed him that we had tapes rolling on all those late-night phone calls he made to his secretary Tiffany.

STEPHEN HADLEY, NATIONAL SECURITY ADVISER

I KNOW THERE'S THIS PERCEPTION that the president doesn't take his role as commander in chief seriously. Nothing could be further from the truth. George W. Bush realizes that sending young men and women into battle is the most solemn, sacred duty afforded a president. He treats this responsibility with a great deal of respect. And because of that, he's earned the respect of the military.

SCOTT McCLELLAN, FORMER WHITE HOUSE PRESS SECRETARY

Do we respect him? Well, he had a cotton candy machine installed in the Situation Room. I'll admit that caused some eyes to roll.

RICHARD MYERS,
FORMER CHAIRMAN OF THE JOINT CHIEFS OF STAFF

I REMEMBER ONE DAY we had a video link-up with General Abizaid in Iraq. We were trying to get a sense of what the situation was on the ground. Honestly, it was a little hard to hear Abizaid because Bush was on the phone with the White House chef screaming, "No! No! No! I wanted *blue* cotton candy!"

DAVID DAUENHEIMER,
FORMER MEMBER OF THE NATIONAL SECURITY COUNCIL

I don't know if it was as a result of the cotton candy mishap, but in February 2005 White House chef Walter Scheib was fired. As Walter was packing up his office, Rumsfeld swung by and said, "I screw up an entire war and yet you're the one who gets fired?!" Rummy was pretty pissed.

ANDY CARD, FORMER CHIEF OF STAFF

I WALKED INTO THE OVAL OFFICE the next day and shoved a wad of blue cotton candy right in Bush's face. The bastard still wouldn't fire me.

DONALD RUMSFELD, FORMER SECRETARY OF DEFENSE

I studied at the Culinary Institute of America. As the White House chef, I assumed I'd be preparing elaborate six-course meals for elegant state dinners. Instead, the bulk of my culinary responsibilities involved pouring something called "Franken Berry" into a bowl. Of course, Franken Berry wasn't the only thing I poured him. Bush was knocking back a fifth of Wild Turkey a day. But then he started to get worried about bird flu, so he switched from Wild Turkey to Beefeater. He said it was his way of "keepin' one step ahead of the chicken man."

WALTER S. SCHEIB III, FORMER WHITE HOUSE EXECUTIVE CHEF

SURE, IT MAY SEEM LIKE all President Bush cares about is cotton candy or Franken Berry, but the reality is he's tremendously involved with the war. I still get goose bumps when I think about a speech President Bush gave to a group of soldiers who were about to be sent off to Iraq. He vowed to those brave young men and women that he wouldn't rest until there was victory in Iraq.

JOSH BOLTEN, CHIEF OF STAFF

Yeah, I remember that speech. He said he wouldn't rest until there was victory in Iraq. Then he got on a plane and flew to Crawford for a month.

George H. W. Bush, former president

It's so unfair to criticize George for taking a little vacation now and then. Those trips to Crawford really keep George centered. Halfway through, you can see him getting a little depressed as he realizes there's only four weeks of vacation left.

Laura Bush, first lady

This isn't a president who spends his vacations sipping white wine on Martha's Vineyard. President Bush spends his vacations the way real Americans do—relaxing on their 1,600-acre private ranch for six or seven weeks.

Karen Hughes, longtime staffer

I realize I'm not the "cool brother." Whenever I try to call George, the switchboard operator transfers me to a recording about how to get tickets to the White House tour. That's why it meant so much to me in August 2005 when George's staff invited me to the ranch for a weekend. It was wonderful! I didn't get to speak to George directly, but I was able to hang out with the Undersecretary of Agriculture's intern. I did get a glimpse of George one night when he hosted a cookout.

Marvin Bush, brother

Yeah, I believe George built the fire with articles of the Constitution he didn't think applied to him.

George H. W. Bush, FORMER PRESIDENT

It was a magical night. The staff asked if I wanted to get my photo taken with George, but unfortunately I didn't have $2,500 on me.

Marvin Bush, BROTHER

It's a time, really, for him to shed the coat and tie and meet with folks out in the heartland and hear what's on their mind.

Scott McClellan,
FORMER WHITE HOUSE PRESS SECRETARY,
DEFENDING PRESIDENT BUSH'S MAMMOTH VACATIONS IN AUGUST 2005

Trespassers will be shot on sight.

CORRECTION ISSUED BY WHITE HOUSE AFTER BEING ASKED FOR DETAILS AS TO WHEN REGULAR "HEARTLAND FOLKS" SHOULD SHOW UP TO THE RANCH TO TELL BUSH WHAT'S ON THEIR MINDS.

Last year President Bush was in Crawford on the weekend when we turned the clocks back. He loved that extra hour of sleep! He wanted to introduce legislation to turn the clocks back again the following weekend. And then another hour the weekend after that. And then two hours on his birthday. Basically, he wanted to take what he's doing with the deficit and apply it to time.

Andy Card, FORMER CHIEF OF STAFF

I DON'T WANT TO REVEAL too much about what the president does while he's on vacation, but let's just say the Secret Service code name for Crawford is "Margaritaville."

BILL DELACE, SECRET SERVICE AGENT

We were so involved with Iraq and vacations that I'll admit we sort of forgot about Osama. But in the summer of 2005 we picked up some chatter about a potential plot in which Osama bin Laden would poison the cocaine coming into the U.S. When we informed the president, he exploded.

PORTER GOSS, FORMER CIA DIRECTOR

PRESIDENT BUSH believes in loyalty—both to people and narcotics. He views cocaine as an old friend, so this plot really hit a nerve.

KARL ROVE, DIRECTOR OF PROPAGANDA

President Bush was screaming, "Now he's gone too far! You don't mess with another man's blow! A man's cocaine stash—that's sacred!" His outburst was a little awkward because it took place while he was hosting a White House T-ball game.

ANDY CARD, FORMER CHIEF OF STAFF

THE CHILDREN WERE PRETTY UPSET. Seven is a little young to see the president screaming, "If that bastard ever touches my blow, I'll rip out his eyeballs and snort cocaine out of his sockets!"

LAURA BUSH, FIRST LADY

CHAPTER 15

Vice Presidents Are Supposed to *Attend* Funerals, Not Cause Them

I never thought, and looking back perhaps I was naive, but I honestly never thought Dick Cheney would shoot me in cold blood.

HARRY WHITTINGTON, FRIEND

IN EARLY 2006 I hosted Dick Cheney on a quail-hunting trip where he accidentally shot his friend. After the shooting, some suggested that Cheney was drunk. I don't know. That's a gray area. Does fifteen beers qualify as "drunk"?

KATHARINE ARMSTRONG, OWNER, ARMSTRONG RANCH

The doctors estimated that Cheney shot Whittington with between six and two hundred pellets. By the same token, Cheney estimated he had had between six and two hundred beers before he went hunting.

LORRAINE GALLER, CHENEY SPOKESPERSON

WE FELT WE SHOULD get ahead of the story by having the vice president give a press conference.

SCOTT MCCLELLAN, FORMER WHITE HOUSE PRESS SECRETARY

When I broached the subject of holding a press conference, the vice president snapped, "If I held a press conference every single time I shot somebody, I'd never get any work done!"

MARY MATALIN, FORMER COUNSELOR TO THE VICE PRESIDENT

BIG DEAL, the vice president shot somebody. That's a one-day story. But the liberal media is so outrageous, they made it a three-day story. For them to attack the vice president—in a time of war, I might add—for something as minor as shooting one meaningless old man is simply unconscionable.

SCOTT MCCLELLAN, FORMER WHITE HOUSE PRESS SECRETARY

People think Dick Cheney is insensitive, but the day after the hunting accident he was at Harry Whittington's hospital. Granted, Cheney went to the hospital because he'd suffered another heart "episode," but he did give Harry a "thumbs up" when they passed each other in the ER.

LEWIS "SCOOTER" LIBBY, CHENEY'S FORMER CHIEF OF STAFF

IN VICE PRESIDENT CHENEY'S DEFENSE, maybe he would have known how to handle a gun if the Democratic-controlled Congress hadn't prevented him from serving his country in Vietnam by allowing him to seek deferments.

LORRAINE GALLER, CHENEY SPOKESPERSON

The press was being vicious toward Dick. Events like this one really show you who your friends are. Unfortunately, Dick learned he didn't have any.

LYNNE CHENEY, WIFE OF THE VICE PRESIDENT

THE WEEK OF THE SHOOTING President Bush was walking around with a big ol' smile. He kept saying, "Hmm, maybe I'm *not* the biggest dumbass in this administration!'

ANDY CARD, FORMER CHIEF OF STAFF

To quell the controversy, the vice president finally agreed to give an interview to Brit Hume on FOX News. It was a smashing success.

SCOTT MCCLELLAN, FORMER WHITE HOUSE PRESS SECRETARY

YEAH, THE WHITE HOUSE deemed it a success. Hey, I'm no PR genius, but if I'm Cheney, I throw on a pair of pants for the interview.

BRIT HUME, FOX NEWS ANCHOR

For weeks after the shooting, Cheney would wander the White House halls screaming that the blood wouldn't come off his hands. It really freaked out some of the tour groups.

ANDY CARD, FORMER CHIEF OF STAFF

We couldn't have the vice president suffering a nervous breakdown in front of tour groups. So we phonied up another terror alert that allowed us to cancel the White House tours.

Michael Chertoff, HOMELAND SECURITY SECRETARY

I was really disappointed. I'd finally gotten tickets and the day before I was supposed to go, they cancelled the tours.

Marvin Bush, BROTHER

Even before the shooting, things between Bush and Cheney had become very strained. I recall one morning informing the president that Cheney had been rushed to the hospital with chest pains. Without even looking up from his Game Boy, President Bush muttered, "Wow, there's a shocker."

Karl Rove, DIRECTOR OF PROPAGANDA

After one particularly heated meeting, the president held up a list of all the people he executed while governor and said, "See what I'm driving at, Dick?"

Colin Powell, FORMER SECRETARY OF STATE

Someone drew devil horns on all the photos of Cheney in the White House hallways. I don't want to make accusations, but President Bush had black ink all over his hands.

Lynne Cheney, WIFE OF THE VICE PRESIDENT

Look, everybody knows Cheney's a jerk. It just took George six years to realize it. [Laughs sarcastically] Oh dear, I sure hope his magical "intuition" isn't on the fritz.

GEORGE H. W. BUSH, FORMER PRESIDENT

[Editor's note: In 2005 Vice President Cheney had surgery to remove an aneurysm in an artery behind his right knee. We talked with his daughter to see how she held up during the medical scare.]

HE HAD AN ANEURYSM in his knee. You believe that?! The son of a bitch is so fat he's having heart attacks in his knee!

MARY CHENEY, LESBIAN DAUGHTER

I'll let you in on a little secret. You know why Cheney does that lip curl thing? He thinks it makes him look like Billy Idol. [Laughs] What a loser.

COLIN POWELL, FORMER SECRETARY OF STATE

CHENEY HAD A NUMBER of enemies in the administration. In fact, there was some thought given to replacing Cheney on the 2004 ticket, but c'mon, where else was Bush gonna find someone with a rock-solid 18 percent approval rating?

MATTHEW DOWD, REPUBLICAN POLLSTER

It seemed whenever Bush tried to fire Cheney, Dick would make up some story about how it was his birthday and you can't fire someone on their birthday. He should be about 180 with all the birthdays he's claimed to have had. Actually, when you look at him, 180 seems about right.

LAURA BUSH, FIRST LADY

MY DAD LOVES TO PRETEND he's Mr. Tough Guy, but he's actually a pansy. He's scared of everything. For instance, he demanded that a bomb shelter be built in his backyard. He also insists that a biohazard suit be with him at all times in case of a chemical attack. If he's so concerned with staying alive, you'd think he might stop eating mozzarella sticks for breakfast.

MARY CHENEY, LESBIAN DAUGHTER

CHAPTER 16

"Hey, 16! Just Like My Approval Rating!"

"Don't Blame Me, I Voted for Kerry"

BUMPER STICKER SPOTTED ON GEORGE H. W. BUSH'S CAR

THE YEAR 2006 began with Cheney shooting a guy. And things got worse from there. We couldn't catch a damn break.

KARL ROVE, DIRECTOR OF PROPAGANDA

During an outdoor press conference June 14, 2006, the president mocked *Los Angeles Times* reporter Peter Wallsten for wearing "shades." The president failed to realize that Wallsten is legally blind.

SCOTT MCCLELLAN,
FORMER WHITE HOUSE PRESS SECRETARY

HE'S BLIND? Oh God, please tell me he's deaf also.

PRESIDENT BUSH UPON BEING TOLD ABOUT WALLSTEN'S CONDITION

The president was very apologetic. He even bought me a gift to say he was sorry. It was a brand-new telescope, which was a lovely gesture, but you know.

Peter Wallsten, REPORTER, *LOS ANGELES TIMES*

AMID ALL THE PROBLEMS, occasionally you'd get one of those magical days that remind you this is the best place to work in the world. For instance, one day Bono came to the White House to discuss global poverty. He looked so cool strolling in wearing his sunglasses. The president took his arm and gently led him into the room while saying how sorry he was to learn Bono was blind. When Bono said he wasn't blind, Bush threw up his hands and sighed, "I freakin' give up!"

Jessica Santini, WHITE HOUSE SPOKESWOMAN

Yeah, presidents have to do that celebrity photo op crap all the time. You've all seen that photo of Nixon with Elvis. In 1992 when "Baby Got Back" was number one, I had to do a photo op with Sir Mix-a-Lot where he was pointing at my ass while giving an "okay" sign. Pathetic. We all do it, but the thing that was different about George and Bono was you had the president of the United States with a rock star and the rock star was the one who's more of a statesman. Tell me we wouldn't be in better shape if Bono was president.

George H. W. Bush, FORMER PRESIDENT

I'M ACTUALLY THINKING about running for president.

BONO, U2 SINGER

[Editor's note: When I informed Bono that the president has to have actually been born in the U.S., Bono dismissed this with a vague promise that he was going to "Rock the Constitution."]

I think a Bono presidency would be pretty good. First off, it might be refreshing to have a president who could actually find Sarajevo on a map. Another thing, despite your nation's glorious history, I don't believe you've ever had a vice president named "The Edge." Most importantly, I could solve your Iraq problem simply by giving my State of the Union while draining a few pints of Guinness. Let's face it, not even the Shiite death squads would want to deal with a drunk Irishman.

BONO, U2 SINGER

AS BAD AS THINGS WERE going in Iraq, President Bush claimed he'd stay there even if Laura and Barney were the only ones supporting him.

BOB WOODWARD, ASSISTANT MANAGING EDITOR, *WASHINGTON POST*

That's true. He'll stay in Iraq even if no one else wants him to. President Bush is steady. He's not going to change his actions because of polls or elections or the will of the people. Changing how you act based on the will of the people sounds dangerously close to "democracy." This president is going to continue doing what he wants because he's a dictat—I mean, he's steady.

KARL ROVE, DIRECTOR OF PROPAGANDA

As much as the president says he doesn't care about polls, the 2006 election really bothered him. When the results came in, he finally had to face the fact that the American people had lost faith in him. He was pretty depressed.

Tony Snow, white house press secretary

George was so depressed it started affecting his sleep. He was down to only ten and a half hours a night. So I suggested he see a psychologist.

Laura Bush, first lady

I was brought in because I have a lot of experience treating celebrities. For instance, I cured Steven Seagal's bed wetting. I also helped Rosie O'Donnell overcome her battle with anorexia.

Dr. Judy Wahrenberger, psychologist

Dr. Wahrenberger helped me get off drugs in 1998. She also helped me get off drugs in 1999 and 2002. And then she helped me get off drugs in 2003, 2004, and 2005.

Courtney Love, rock star

I had just about cured his depression over the election, when the Iraq Study Group's report came out.

Dr. Judy Wahrenberger, psychologist

Yeah, the Iraq Study Group's report sent him over the edge. He was so depressed, he made a call to Baghdad asking if he could borrow Saddam's noose when they were done with it.

Tony Snow, WHITE HOUSE PRESS SECRETARY

At least *I* have an exit strategy out of Iraq.

Saddam Hussein'S FINAL WORDS

As happy as we were about Saddam's execution, we were still frustrated by our inability to bring Osama to justice.

Condoleezza Rice, SECRETARY OF STATE

Cheney was particularly haunted by our inability to capture Osama. He'd wander around the White House at all hours of the night muttering Osama's name.

Louise Comey, WHITE HOUSE USHER

Obsessed with Osama? Perhaps. But in the end, my obsession is what enabled me to finally catch him. You see, with Osama it was personal. Even after capturing him, I still wasn't satisfied. Spending eternity in a prison cell was too good for him. So late one night I decided to give him the punishment he deserved. I went down to the cell and told the security guards to take the rest of the night off. I walked into the cold, dark cell where it was just Osama and me. I started him off with a couple lefts to his face. And then when he brought up his hands to protect himself, I worked the body. All you could hear was the crunch of his ribs snapping and his pathetic sobs as I bloodied him. I beat him until he renounced terrorism. I beat him until he renounced Allah. I beat him until he renounced ungrateful lesbian daughters who mock everything their fathers hold dear. When he was good and bloody and begging for mercy, I handed him a piece of paper with the lyrics to my favorite song. I told him, "Sing it, bitch!" With all apologies to Lee Greenwood, I'll never hear a sweeter sound than Osama singing the words "God bless the U.S.A.!"

DICK CHENEY, VICE PRESIDENT

[Editor's note: Uhh, where to begin? We really have no idea what he's talking about here.]

WE HEARD A LOT of banging and screams of "Die Osama!" coming from Vice President Cheney's bunker. We burst in and found Cheney punching himself in the face while singing "God Bless the U.S.A."

MIKE MCINTEE, SECRET SERVICE AGENT

I am Osama; Osama is I.

DICK CHENEY'S STATEMENT TO THE AGENTS WHO DISCOVERED HIM

THE VICE PRESIDENT was clearly exhausted, so we decided to send him to Bethesda Hospital for a nice, long rest.

JOSH BOLTEN, CHIEF OF STAFF

President Bush has really had an interesting life when you look at it all. For twelve years while his dad was in the White House, George had a front-row seat for so many historical moments. And when all is said and done, he'll have been president for eight incredibly momentous years in our nation's history. When you think about it, George is almost like Forrest Gump in the knack he's had for being there during so many remarkable moments. Let me clarify that. George is like a slightly *dumber* version of Forrest Gump.

Professor Patty Carlson, HARVARD UNIVERSITY

I GUESS I SAID some pretty harsh things about George in this book. Thankfully, because it's a book, he'll never see it.

George H. W. Bush, FORMER PRESIDENT

So you want to know some things about George W. Bush that no one else does? Wow, that's a hard one. Let's see. Well, he has a lucky red tie that he likes me to lay out whenever he has a big speech. Also, every year on my birthday, he gets me a dozen yellow Texas roses. He's so sweet. He always tells me that his heart belongs to me—unless, of course, Cheney ever needs it. George is such a wonderful husband. He realizes that marriage requires hard work—unlike the presidency. What else? Well, when he tells the staff he's reading intelligence reports in the residence, he's usually watching baseball. Whenever the Padres are on, he loves dressing up as that San Diego Chicken. You might not know this, but a year ago I told George we should register the domain name www.impeachbush.com to make sure the Democrats didn't get it. But between you and me, I've begun collecting signatures for the site. What else can I tell you about him? Well, not *everything's* big in Texas if you catch my drift. And he may go around pretending he's Mr. Man, but let's just say there hasn't been a "Mission Accomplished" sign hanging above our bed in two years. Wow, get me a piña colada—this is fun!

Laura Bush, FIRST LADY

Acknowledgments

I'd like to thank all the White House officials and Bush confidants for speaking with me. I owe a particular debt of gratitude to former President George H. W. Bush for being so candid with the criticisms of his son. I know it wasn't easy, sir. And while we're at it, thanks to George W. Bush. All kidding aside, I really think he's starting to get the hang of it.

Here's how good an agent Daniel Greenberg is—he took a guy who can barely read (me!) and got him a book deal. I appreciate your efforts; you remain in my thoughts, sir. I also want to thank Chris Schillig and all the fine folks at Andrews McMeel, such as Michelle Daniel, for turning my bizarre ramblings into an actual book. A West Coast "shout out" to David Miner, the finest manager since Billy Martin. And thanks to Jay Johnson for the sizzling stalkerazzi photo.

Gerry Mulligan, Walter Kim, and Lorraine Galler all read an early draft and gave me invaluable advice. I'm very lucky to have such smart, gracious friends. Speaking of good friends, you can't do much better than Wally, Nancy, Jay, the Schukeis, Bob, Billy, Rich, and Alden. And in this corner, thanks to Foley, Sheryl, Paula, and Lorraine for all the boozy Thursday nights.

A big "what up" to everyone at the Late Show—Eric, Justin, Joe, Jeremy, Lee, Steve, Meredith, Bob, and Scheft are a darn funny group to spend your day with; thanks to the rest of the gang on fourteen; Mark, Steve, Andrew, and Dava for saving me countless times under